IMAGES
of America

SUNRIVER

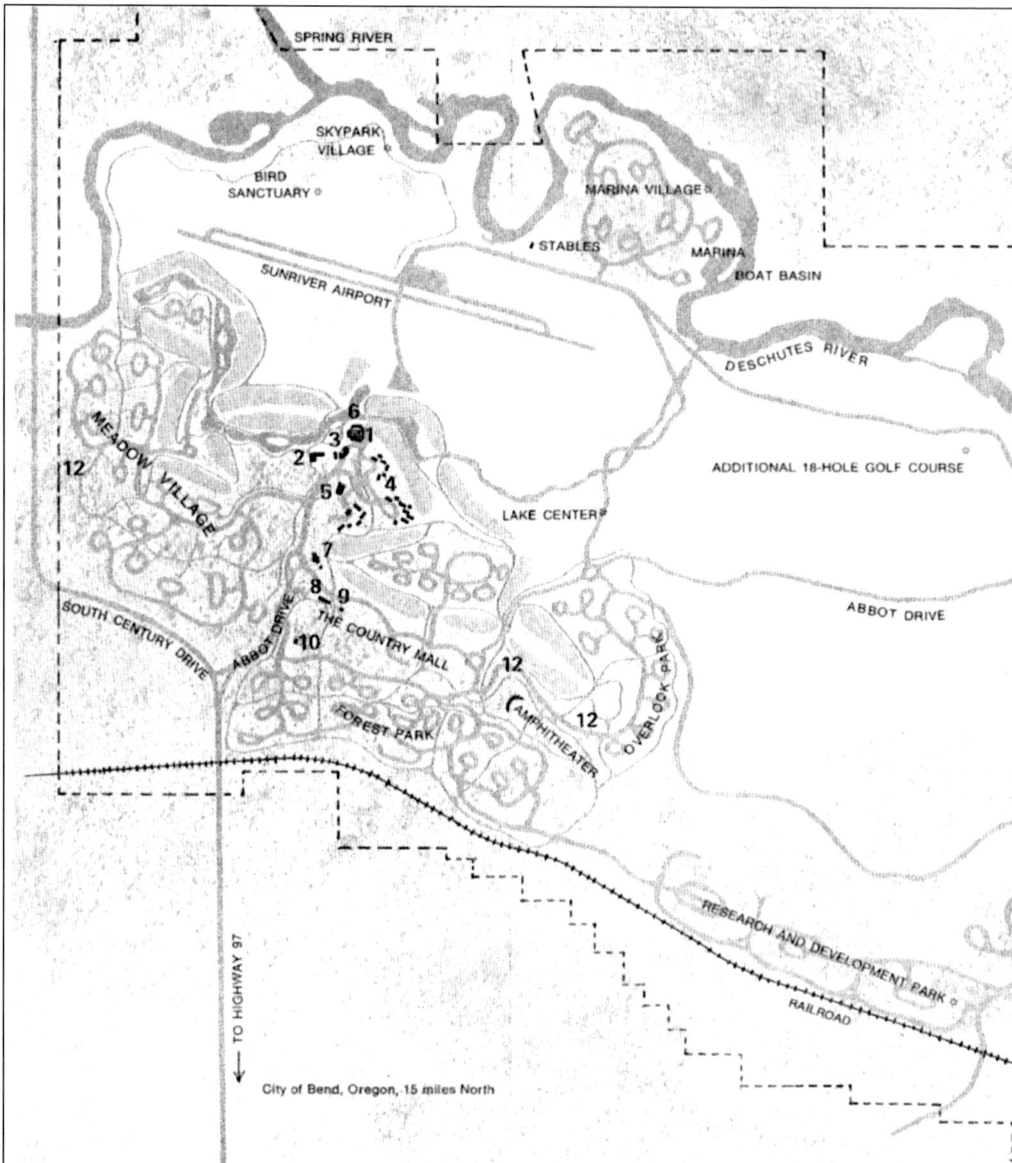

This map of Sunriver was published in the early 1970s. The familiar landmarks are already in place: The Sunriver Lodge (No. 1 on the map), The Great Hall (No. 2), South Pool (No. 3), the Country Store (No. 10), and completed condominium clusters (No. 12). The south course (later renamed Woodlands) weaves through the Sunriver core areas. (Courtesy of Sunriver Resort.)

On the Cover: This publicity shot for Sunriver Properties from 1978 features a plethora of recreational activities available for visitors to Sunriver Resort. The photograph was taken on the tarmac at the airport looking south. Sunriver Lodge is visible in the background. (Courtesy of Sunriver Resort.)

IMAGES
of America

SUNRIVER

Tor Hanson

ARCADIA
PUBLISHING

ISBN 978-1-4671-2993-0

Published by Arcadia Publishing
Charleston, South Carolina

Printed in the United States of America

Library of Congress Control Number: 2018949071

For all general information, please contact Arcadia Publishing:
Telephone 843-853-2070
Fax 843-853-0044
E-mail sales@arcadiapublishing.com
For customer service and orders:
Toll-Free 1-888-313-2665

Visit us on the Internet at www.arcadiapublishing.com

This book is dedicated to my daughters, Chandra and Viveca, who call my research projects "Playing with the dead people."

Contents

ACKNOWLEDGMENTS

This book project was suggested by Susan Berger, communications director with the Sunriver Owners Association (SROA). I had just finished Images of America: *Camp Abbot* when Susan dropped me a line and asked if I was interested in pursuing a book about Sunriver. "Of course I am interested," I told her.

After completing *Camp Abbot*, I realized the story about this crossroads of Oregon was not fully told. People have inhabited this area since the end of the Ice Age, which ended approximately 11,700 years ago. I needed to take a step further back in time to explain why native tribes, explorers, and homesteaders found the area the perfect place to put down roots, whether migratory or permanent.

I have had plenty of help during the research of this book. My wife, Nancy, is a "first reader" on all my projects, whether articles or books. Beyond spelling and grammar, she lets me know if there are things that do not make sense. I trust her instincts.

My fellow writer and good friend Les Joslin was also along for this project. He helped me proofread the manuscript. Susan Berger was also on the proofreading team.

I also want to thank Kelly Cannon-Miller, Vanessa Ivey, and Shey Hyatt at the Deschutes Historical Museum. They have given me access to the museum's incredible resources, housed at the old Reid School in Bend. Among the collections are thousands of historical photographs from the area, as well as a depository of negatives and color transparencies from *The Bulletin* covering the late 1960s and into the late 1980s.

Susan opened the SROA archives and let me read old *Harold* newsletters and the *Sunriver Scene*, the association's monthly newspaper since 1987. I also found an abundance of photos in their archives, detailing everything that had to do with Sunriver.

Unless otherwise noted, the photographs in this book are courtesy of the Sunriver Owners Association. Images courtesy of the Deschutes Historical Museum are credited as DHM throughout the text.

INTRODUCTION

Central Oregon was not always a high desert with meadows, large stands of timber, and flowing rivers. Evidence suggests that in prehistoric times, the area was covered with lakes and a swamp-like environment. Mastodons even roamed the area.

The Central Oregon high desert is the northern part of the Great Basin, an area that includes Oregon, Idaho, Utah, Nevada, and California. Paleo-Indian habitation began as the Ice Age ended, geologically classified as the Pleistocene period.

According to University of Oregon archeologist Luther Cressman, who explored many of the caves in the area in the late 1930s, evidence suggests the area was inhabited by native tribes as early as 12,750 years ago. Typical hunter/gatherer societies, these tribes may have hunted camel, bison, horse, small mammals, and waterfowl, in addition to collecting edible roots and seeds.

The cool and wet climate that existed in the Northern Great Basin around the end of the Ice Age slowly became warmer and drier. As Cressman and his team of students continued to study the area, they recovered 75 sandals made of sagebrush and bark cords along with arrow points, as well as a large number of stone tools. The findings suggested a healthy establishment of people in the period 12,000–10,000 years ago.

Human habitation came to a screeching halt when Mount Mazama (today known as Crater Lake) erupted approximately 7,500 years ago, turning the fertile marsh and lake area into a wasteland covered by thick layers of ash, at points near the volcano reaching 20 feet deep. In the Fort Rock area, Cressman encountered almost a foot of Mazama ash.

As life returned to the ash-covered high desert, the climate shifted from warm, dry conditions to cooler, wetter weather. By now, approximately 6,000–3,000 years ago, marshes and lakes, ideal conditions for human settlement, covered the area. The native tribes took on a more sedentary lifestyle, evidenced by remnants of houses and storage pits found in the Northern Great Basin area. There is also evidence of active trade between tribes.

During the last approximately 3,000 years, the native tribes inhabiting the northern part of the Great Basin encountered erratic conditions ranging from drought to floods. Between 2,000–200 years ago, the Central Oregon tribes we know today were established—the Molala, Klamath, Modoc, Northern Paiute, Tenino, and Tygh. The area also became part of trade routes from settlements along the Columbia River near The Dalles to tribes living around the Klamath Falls basin.

First contact between the native tribes and Euro-Americans took place approximately 200 years ago. The first white men arrived in the Central Oregon area in 1824. Fur trappers and explorers such as Peter Skene Ogden, John C. Frémont, and Henry Larcom Abbot described the region for future settlement by homesteaders from east of the Mississippi. The Oregon Territory was created in 1848, and Oregon became a state in 1859.

As homestead acts were passed by Congress during the latter 19th and early 20th centuries, suitable Upper Deschutes River lands were settled. Farmers and ranchers like the Shonquests, the Vandeverts, and other land claimants settled the area around the future site of Sunriver.

The Deschutes River was, and is, the key to successful human settlement and occupation of Central Oregon. From its Little Lava Lake headwaters at an elevation of 4,744 feet, the spring-fed river tumbles over eight wild and scenic miles toward Crane Prairie Reservoir, after which the river continues to flow into Wickiup Reservoir.

Farming and irrigation go hand in hand. For anything to grow in the high desert landscape of Central Oregon, farmers need a reliable water source. Dams and reservoirs were the solution. Crane Prairie Dam was constructed in 1922 and rebuilt as a Great Depression project of the US Bureau of Reclamation in 1940. The Wickiup Dam, a larger Bureau of Reclamation project begun during the Depression, impounded the Wickiup Reservoir, Oregon's second largest reservoir. This "Deschutes Project" dam and reservoir were completed in 1949 and then transferred to the North Unit Irrigation District. After passing through these reservoirs, the Deschutes River takes a northeasterly turn to flow past Sunriver.

In July 1929, seven years after the construction of Crane Prairie Dam, members of the Bend and Redmond Chambers of Commerce and Jefferson County Commercial Club, local businessmen, and attorneys tried to persuade the federal government to construct the Benham Falls Reservoir to provide additional storage of irrigation water to help farmers through dry spells. It would also make the return of Lake Benham a reality, turning a large area back to the state it existed in about 6,000 years ago.

Robert W. Sawyer, president of the Bend Chamber of Commerce and publisher of *The Bend Bulletin*, mentioned in a July 1929 front-page article, "It has become apparent in the last few weeks that the whole valley is suffering from a serious water shortage."

It would take the economic downturn of the Depression before the federal government considered the Benham Falls project. Pres. Franklin D. Roosevelt had signaled a keen interest in starting up public works and financial assistance for states and municipalities around the country.

Although the area behind Benham Falls was an old lakebed, there were lingering issues regarding the structural integrity of the area—could the proposed dam hold water?

In early 1934, the US government put forth $50,000 to test the area. Money was funneled through the Public Works Administration, a government agency that concentrated its efforts on shoring up the nation's infrastructure. The drilling started in late May 1934 and continued throughout the summer. A second survey crew worked around the Pringle Falls area in case the Benham Falls site was deemed unfavorable.

After several days of work, the survey crews stopped drilling at "Damsite A." US Bureau of Reclamation hydraulics engineer E.B. Debler characterized the Benham Falls site as "very dubious." Debler had tested the site by pumping 80 gallons of water per minute for 36 hours. By the end of the test, there was no water in the pit, indicating that water had seeped out through porous material far below the surface.

This test effectively ended the Benham Falls Reservoir debate, at least for the time being. Eventually, test drilling around Pringle Falls proved that area could hold a dam just below Crane Prairie dam; between 1939 and 1949, the Wickiup Dam was completed. The Wickiup Reservoir was filled to supply irrigation water via the North Unit canal to the large agricultural area around Madras, Oregon.

The debate about turning the area behind Benham Falls into a reservoir did not fully go away. As late as 1959, the topic was up for debate again. This time the representatives from the different Central Oregon irrigation districts were met by opposition from citizens who believed that the Deschutes had a greater future value than growing crops. Opposing the development of Benham Falls Reservoir were sportsmen and citizens who supported recreational use of the river.

Francis Stokesberry, who represented the Deschutes Sportsmen's Association, said "the Deschutes river above Bend is a great asset." He estimated the loss of land due to the damming of the river above Benham Falls at 7,000 to 8,000 acres.

It was in this setting that the three founders of Sunriver stepped into the foreground. Instead of a place to store irrigation water, the land around what would eventually become Sunriver was left undisturbed.

One

Native Tribes, Explorers, and Homesteaders

Lava Butte, seven miles south of Bend along Highway 97, played an important role in the development of the area around today's Sunriver. A fairly recent addition to the Central Oregon landscape, an eruption created the cinder cone approximately 7,000 years ago. As molten lava from the volcano traveled northwest, it dammed the Deschutes River, creating a 15-mile long lake called Lake Benham.

Paired with climate changes that occurred between 6,000 and 3,000 years ago, the Central Oregon area flourished. The region went from an arid landscape to being wetter and cooler. The large lake and marshland created ideal living conditions for the tribes inhabiting the area. Hunters and fishermen inhabiting the area took full advantage of what the lake and its surroundings provided. With plentiful food sources around the lake, the tribes transformed from a migratory to a sedentary society. Archeological evidence from this period includes permanent structures such as large houses and storage pits.

Climate changes during the last 3,000 years and the disappearance of Lake Benham again changed the population patterns around the area that would eventually become Sunriver. After the river carved a new channel and drained the lake, the area was turned back to meadowland and an ever-expanding forest.

Euro-American fur traders and explorers filtered through the area in the early 19th century, establishing contact with the tribes. Recorded exploration parties in Central Oregon include Peter Skene Ogden, Nathaniel Wyeth, John Frémont, and Henry Larcom Abbot.

The Wasco, Tenino (Warm Springs), and Paiute tribes were displaced from their traditional lands and relegated to reservations. In 1855, a treaty between the US government and the tribes established the Warm Springs Indian Reservation.

Within a short time after Oregon gained statehood in 1859, homesteaders began arriving in Central Oregon, brought there by the Homestead Act of 1862. Farmers, cattle ranchers, and sheepherders filed their 160-acre land claims along the Deschutes River, lured by the promise of fertile lands, readily available irrigation water, and easy living.

Southeast of Sunriver, Fort Rock stands as a testament to Oregon's geological past. The volcanic tuff ring was formed about 50,000–100,000 years ago when a large Ice Age lake covered Central Oregon. A settler of the area, William Sullivan, named the volcanic landmark in 1873, taking cues from the tall rock walls that resemble the palisades of a fort.

Fort Rock Cave is located approximately one-and-a-half miles east of Fort Rock volcanic monument. Alternatively called "Cow Cave" or "Menkimer Cave," the cave was explored by University of Oregon archeologist Luther Cressman and his students in 1938. During the excavations, they found numerous artifacts that proved people had lived there long before the area was thought to have been inhabited.

During that 1938 field season, Cressman and his party dug through several feet of manure and ash. There was a good reason for that Cow Cave name; cattle had sought shelter there for decades. The team discovered more than 70 pairs of sandals as well as other artifacts, including projectile points, stone tools, and part of a basket. At the time, archeologists believed people had not lived in the area longer than 4,000 years. Cressman's findings proved people lived there before the eruption of Mount Mazama, more than 7,000 years ago. Radiocarbon tests in the 1950s verified the sandals were about 9,000 years old. This more than doubled estimates of how long people had lived in the Great Basin and put Oregon prehistory on the map. (Above, courtesy of DHM; below, courtesy of Oregon Historical Society.)

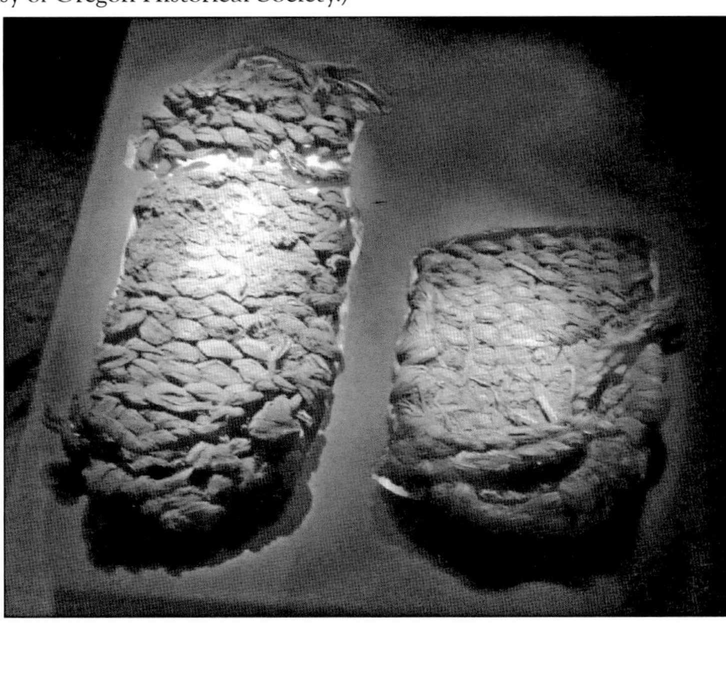

Centuries before Euro-American exploration and settlement of the lands surrounding today's Sunriver, Native American tribes from the sagebrush steppes to the east visited the open Deschutes country each year. Following seasonal hunting and gathering opportunities, they camped along the Deschutes River and on the banks of the 17-mile-long Lake Benham, formed some 6,000 years ago when Lava Butte's lava flow dammed the Deschutes River at Benham Butte. When the lake filled, it went over the top of the dam. When it came in contact with the softer Benham Butte rocks, the water eventually cut the channel now called Benham Falls. (Both, courtesy of DHM.)

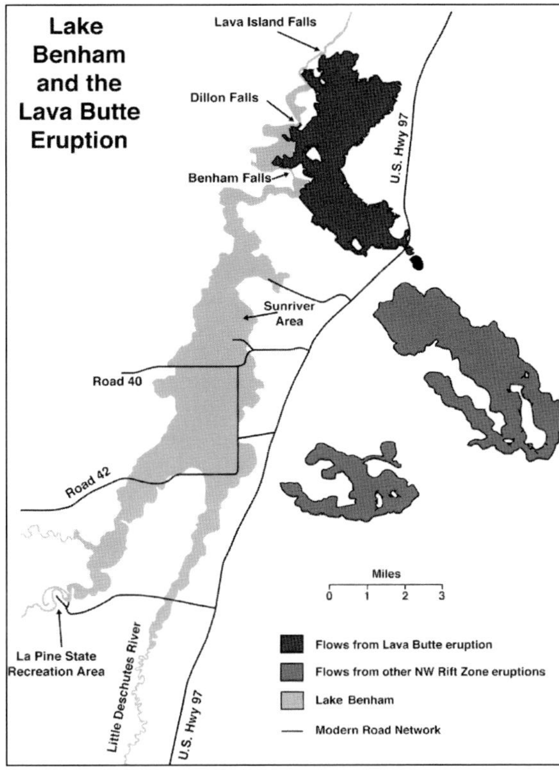

North of Benham Falls, the Deschutes River flows northwest along the western margin of the Lava Butte lava flow. Dillon Falls, named for settler Leander Dillon, is an impressive whitewater cascade about six miles north of Sunriver, where whitewater canoeing and rafting are both deadly and prohibited. (Below, courtesy of DHM.)

Peter Skene Ogden (1790–1854), a Canadian fur trapper and trader in the employ of the Hudson Bay Company, explored much of British Columbia and the American West. Two of his expeditions took him to Central Oregon. His first expedition (1825–1826) followed the Deschutes River inland from the Columbia River. His second Oregon expedition (1826–1827) passed through today's Newberry National Monument along the Deschutes River to Klamath Falls. (Courtesy of DHM.)

Nathaniel Jarvis Wyeth (1802–1856) was an inventor and businessman from Cambridge, Massachusetts. Through his involvement with promoter Hall Jackson Kelly, who hoped to colonize Oregon, he put together an expedition in 1832. The first expedition was plagued by setbacks. After returning home in 1833, Wyeth planned a new expedition. In December 1834, he and his men camped on the future site of Bend and portaged around Benham Falls on their travels as far up the Deschutes River as Pringle Falls. (Courtesy of DHM.)

Capt. John Charles Frémont (1831–1927), US Army Corps of Topographical Engineers, explored the area in 1843. His original mission was to map the second part of the Oregon Trail, paving the way for thousands of settlers. During the expedition, Frémont decided to do some freelance work to explore the Great Basin. During his travels along the eastern flank of the Cascades, the party passed by Dillon Falls and Benham Falls. (Courtesy of DHM.)

The next major exploration of the area came in September 1855. A young lieutenant, Henry Larcom Abbot, and a team of Pacific Railroad survey engineers from the US Army Corps of Topographical Engineers forded the Deschutes River on September 2 and camped within the future boundaries of the US Army Corps of Engineers training center that would be named for him. Abbot retired as a brigadier general. (Courtesy of DHM.)

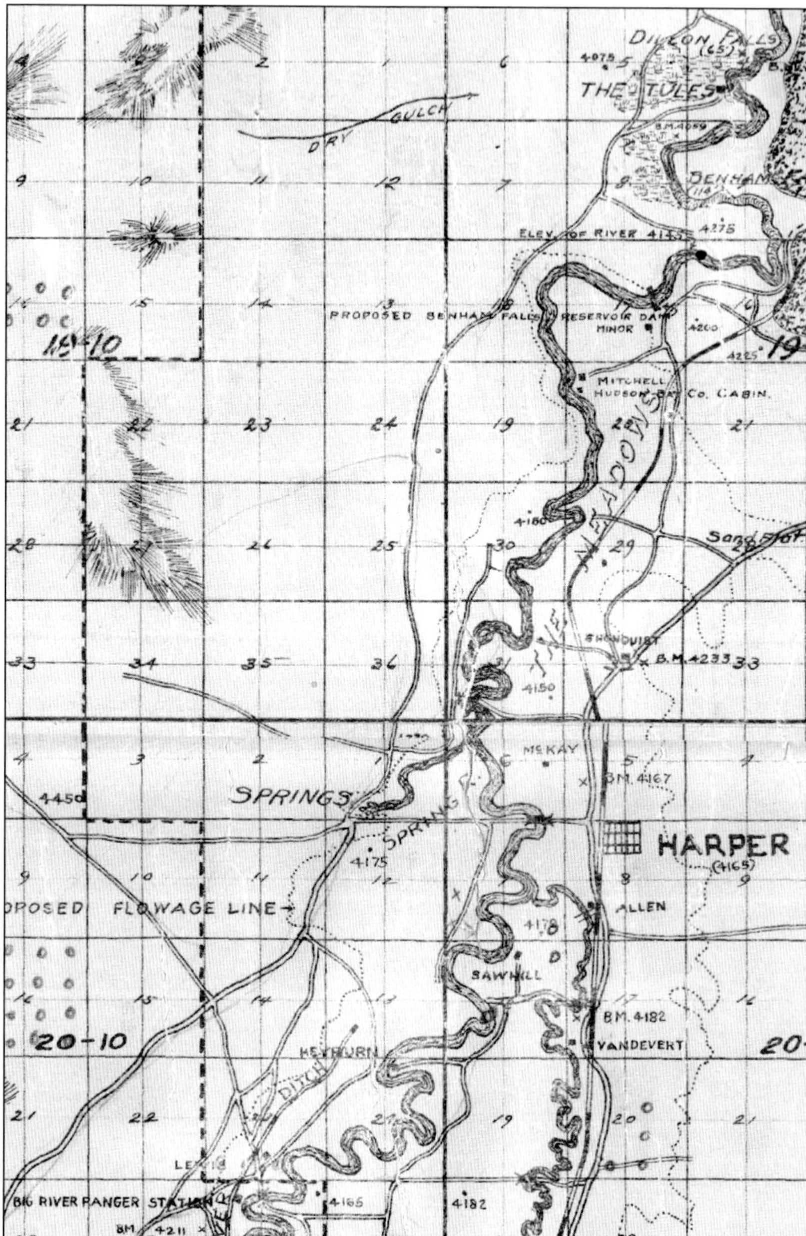

Once Native American hunting grounds, the area changed little until the late 19th century, when various homestead acts encouraged settlers to claim land. The meadow became home to several homesteads on which settlers grazed their livestock. This 1915 map by Bend city engineer Robert Gould shows the locations of the Shonquest Ranch, the McKay homestead, and the Vandevert Ranch along the Deschutes River as it snakes northward toward Benham Falls. Also on the map is the platted townsite of Harper, Oregon, a town that did not exist beyond Gould's map. The Shonquest Ranch was located on the old Huntington Wagon Road. Named for J.W. Perit Huntington, superintendent of Indian affairs for Oregon, the road opened in 1867 as a supply route between the US Army outpost of Fort Dalles on the Columbia River and Fort Klamath, between Crater Lake and Upper Klamath Lake in Klamath County.

Clyde McKay and his father, Duncan L. McKay (pictured), came to Bend in 1900. Originally a timber cruiser for two Minnesota lumber companies, Shevlin-Hixon and Brooks-Scanlon, Clyde was one of the founders of the Bend Company, which operated a small sawmill on the banks of the Deschutes River where Columbia Park in Bend is today. (Courtesy of DHM.)

Fred and Annie Shonquest arrived in Central Oregon in the early 1900s. The first mention of the Shonquests is an ad in *The Bend Bulletin* in late October 1904, when Fred managed the Minnesota Buffet in Bend. Shonquest became one of the first elected members of the city council. In March 1912, he patented his homestead claim on the land just north of Sunriver where Overlook Road is today. (Courtesy of DHM.)

William P. Vandevert was born in the Willamette Valley in 1854. He, his wife, Sadie, and their family eventually settled in Central Oregon, building Vandevert Ranch in 1892. Expanded over the years, the ranch served as an early stage stop, and in 1898, the Lava Post Office was established on their ranch. The Vandevert kids went to school at Big Meadows School District No. 34, which was organized on July 27, 1887. The school was located on the Aldridge homestead, close to where Sunriver's Great Hall is today. Pictured below are, from left to right, (first row) Maude Vandevert, Clint Vandevert, Goldie West, Leona Aldridge, Carrie Fee (teacher), Iva West, Madie Aldridge, Bill Vandevert, and George Vandevert; (second row) Grace Vandevert, Eva West, and Claude Vandevert. (Both, courtesy of DHM.)

Two

Deschutes National Forest and Lumber Companies

Sunriver is virtually surrounded by Deschutes National Forest lands, managed by the US Forest Service, an agency of the US Department of Agriculture. Established in 1908, this national forest has been headquartered in Bend since 1911. After an early history of custodianship that primarily involved protecting the forest from fire and trespass, more recently, multiple use management has characterized Deschutes National Forest management in support of Central Oregon's economy.

Minnesota lumber companies Shevlin-Hixon and Brooks-Scanlon bought up large parcels of land between 1890 and 1910. By 1914, the Shevlin interests in Oregon tallied 230,000 acres. Brooks-Scanlon's holdings were estimated at approximately 50,000–60,000 acres.

Bend was a boomtown in the early 1910s. The long-anticipated railroad arrived in 1911. With the advent of the railroad, an abundance of timber, and the coming of the Shevlin-Hixon and Brooks-Scanlon mills, Bend was poised to become a "real" town.

The two companies each built a huge mill on opposite sides of the Deschutes River. They were a marvel of engineering. Everything both companies had learned when it came to lumbering went into the mills.

The two Bend sawmills had an unquenchable appetite for lumber. In 1917, one year after starting up operations in Bend, Shevlin-Hixon cut 103 million board feet of lumber, while Brooks-Scanlon cut 65 million, an incredible amount of lumber in a town where the closest competitor, the Pine Tree Lumber Company, cut 7 million feet of lumber in one year.

During the Roaring Twenties, the two Bend mills were the two largest pine mills in the United States. Statistics tell the story: In 1924, the two mills maintained an average production of 207 million feet. In 1925, they produced 360 million feet, and in 1926, they produced 307 million feet.

In the process, the large lumber companies cut all their privately owned timberlands and eventually had to turn to the Deschutes National Forest for logs to support their mills and sustain the local timber-based economy.

By the early 1950s, the large timber stands were depleted. The last log went through the Shevlin-Hixon mill in December 1950. With that, the golden age of logging in Bend was over.

Gifford Pinchot, the first American trained as a forester, worked with Pres. Theodore Roosevelt to establish the Forest Service in the US Department of Agriculture in 1905. Administration of the forest reserves, in the hands of the General Land Office of the US Department of the Interior, was transferred to the Forest Service in 1905, and in 1907, the forest reserves were renamed national forests. (Courtesy of US Forest Service.)

The timber, water forage, and wildlife resources of Central Oregon were appreciated by early conservationists as well as settlers and developers. Gifford Pinchot, then a 36-year-old chief of the Bureau of Forestry in the US Department of Agriculture, took this photograph of Benham Falls on the Deschutes River just north of today's Sunriver in August 1901. (Courtesy of US Forest Service.)

The sawmills' appetite for lumber was insatiable. Bend's huge Brooks-Scanlon and Shevlin-Hixon lumber companies started operations in 1916, and within a decade, they had cut over most of their timber holdings. To sustain their logging operations and the local economy, the lumber companies approached Deschutes National Forest officials for relief. As authorized by the General Exchange Act of 1922, the federal government allowed private companies to exchange their cutover lands for the right to cut national forest timber under the supervision of the US Forest Service. The mostly cutover timberlands around what eventually became Sunriver went from private ownership to being a part of the Deschutes National Forest in a matter of a decade. (Both, courtesy of DHM.)

The annual Shevlin-Hixon picnic became a mainstay of Bend summer activities in 1920. Every person in Bend was invited to attend, whether a Shevlin-Hixon Lumber company employee or not. The entire city closed down. Guests were treated to food, drinks (lemonade and water; this

Folks were transported to a Benham Falls picnic area on the company's logging railroads, everybody enjoying an open-air ride aboard railroad flatcars normally used for transporting logs. (Courtesy of DHM.)

was during Prohibition), ice cream, and candy for the kids. Throughout the day, there were events such as pie-eating contests, three-legged races, sack races, a greased pig battle, and a tug-of-war between the mill workers and the woodsmen. (Courtesy of DHM.)

The 40-man-strong Shevlin-Hixon Company lumberjack band was founded in January 1920. Strongly supported by the mill, the band enjoyed uniforms and instruments purchased by the company. At the third annual Shevlin-Hixon picnic in 1922, the employee band entertained more than 2,000 guests as they climbed aboard the train, and later during the lunch hour. (Courtesy of DHM.)

In 1944, Deschutes National Forest supervisor Ralph Crawford inspects ponderosa pine trees planted by Bend High School students in 1940 on former private timberlands added to the national forest under the General Exchange Act of 1922. Neither the Brooks-Scanlon nor Shevlin-Hixon companies practiced sustained-yield forestry, instead opting to "cut out and get out." The few trees left in the wake of this cutting proved insufficient seed sources to establish new timber stands, and supplemental hand planting of seedlings was necessary. The ponderosa pine timberlands surrounding Sunriver today are second-growth forest and are managed by the Forest Service to produce a sustainable supply of timber. (Courtesy of US Forest Service.)

Three

Camp Abbot

The United States was woefully unprepared for World War II. Although the war had raged for two years in Europe, the American armed forces counted a mere 1.8 million men. That all ended with Japan's surprise attack on Pearl Harbor on December 7, 1941, which drew the United States into the war.

As the country embarked on an unprecedented military buildup, the US Army Corps of Engineers realized the need for additional training centers. The corps already operated two training centers east of the Mississippi, one at Fort Belvoir, Virginia, and one at Fort Leonard Wood, Missouri, but the need for additional engineers to replace those wounded or killed was dire.

Brig. Gen. Clarence Sturdevant of the Corps of Engineers suggested placing a training center on the West Coast. Col. Richard Park, division engineer for the North Pacific division with headquarters in Portland, was well acquainted with Central Oregon and suggested the area around the Shonquest Ranch south of Bend on the Deschutes River. The future site of Sunriver seemed similar to the European landscape in which combat engineers would operate.

Officials in Washington, DC, approved the new Engineer Replacement Training Center (ERTC) in October 1942. Robert W. Sawyer, publisher of *The Bend Bulletin* and a history buff, suggested the name Camp Abbot in honor of the late Brig. Gen. Henry Larcom Abbot, a US Army Corp of Engineers member of a Pacific Railroad survey party. The surveyors came through the Central Oregon area in early fall 1855 and camped in the general vicinity of the future Camp Abbot on September 2. The name of the ERTC was approved in December 1942.

Construction of Camp Abbot began on December 14, 1942. Led by Lt. Col. Alfred D. Harvey, the construction crews consisted of a 500-person detachment of military and civilian personnel.

With a hard delivery date of May 1, 1943, set by Secretary of War Henry L. Stimson, it was quite the achievement that Camp Abbot stood move-in ready after only five months of work. Construction included over 50 barracks, administration buildings, office space for civilian employees, mess halls, recreation facilities, laundry facilities, and a 400-bed hospital. In addition, contractors built all infrastructure such as water, sewer, and electricity.

Camp Abbot opened on schedule. On that day, a contingent of 250 soldiers arrived at the ERTC.

The history of the US Army Corps of Engineers goes back to 1775 when the Continental Congress appointed Col. Richard Gridley as its first chief engineer. French engineers seconded by King Louis XVI to Gen. George Washington during the Revolutionary War originally staffed the corps. The corps' castle insignia, reflected in Camp Abbot's entrance, derives from one of the gates of the city of Verdun, France. (US Army Signal Corps.)

Col. Frank S. Besson and his staff took command of the ERTC on May 9, 1943. Pictured from left to right are (first row) Lt. Col. C.J. Douglas, Col. L. Hall, Colonel Besson, and Lt. Col. Merril Pimentel; (second row) Maj. Paul Diediker, Maj. Terrill, Maj. M.J. Cuadra, Capt. A.A. English, and Lt. W.F. Pascoe. (US Army Signal Corps.)

Work on Camp Abbot began in December 1942 and continued until May 1, 1943, when it was turned over to the US Army. The military installation provided housing for 10,000 troops in over 50 barracks. In addition, soldiers and civilian contractors built administration buildings, mess halls, recreation facilities, chapels, storage facilities, and a hospital with 400 beds. (US Army Signal Corps.)

On May 18, 1943, Camp Abbot celebrated the first official raising of the garrison flag. Speaking briefly, Colonel Besson said the dedication of the camp would happen on either August 12, the 112th anniversary of Brig. Gen. Henry Larch Abbot's birth, or on September 2, to celebrate the fording of the Deschutes River by the Pacific Railroad survey engineers in 1855. (Courtesy of US Army Signal Corps.)

The first contingent of soldiers arrived at Camp Abbot on May 1, 1943. As the ERTC approached full strength, the training of incoming citizens began. Over 900 replacement engineers completed their training every two weeks. The task of turning civilians into soldiers fell on the drill sergeant. Many soldiers can attest to the fact that the tough-as-nails training staff became either their best friend or worst enemy. Colonel Besson drove home a simple message to soldiers at Camp Abbot: "Sweat Saves Blood." Physical conditioning also started immediately. Trainees were sent on marches throughout the rugged high desert terrain. Depending on the season, the soldiers had to deal with dust, mud, or snow. The long, dry summer months made day marches a challenge. The red dust penetrated everything and made even breathing difficult. (Both, courtesy of US Army Signal Corps.)

After turning raw recruits into soldiers, the next step for Camp Abbot's instructors was specialist training. Based on their performance in basic training and their aptitudes, soldiers were assigned to training companies to become cooks, carpenters, automotive mechanics, heavy equipment operators, or demolition crew members. Men without aptitudes for these specialties received training as combat engineers. They had to be ready for anything the enemy had to offer. They had to learn to build anything from simple rope-tow bridges for troops to cross a small stream to pontoon bridges that could carry tanks and troop transport convoys. The engineers also had to learn to destroy bridges to stop enemy troop movements and build emergency anti-tank ditches. After successfully completing training at Camp Abbot, the engineers were shipped off to Europe and took part in many important battles on the way to Berlin. (Both, courtesy of US Army Signal Corps.)

The largest single construction project in the history of Camp Abbot was the officers' mess. Colonel Besson envisioned the project only three weeks after the official opening of the ERTC. Designed by Capt. John Banks, construction of the new officers' mess began in earnest in October 1943. Classified as a training project, construction took six months. Along the way, most Camp Abbot trainees were involved. Building materials for the mountain-style lodge were sourced locally. The first and only major event at the officers' mess, held before it was completed, was a well-attended New Year's party for Camp Abbot's officers and their families. The officers' mess was completed in April 1944 and dedicated on April 29 with all the pomp and circumstance worthy of an official building. Below is the Great Hall. (Above, courtesy of US Army Signal Corps; below, courtesy of DHM.)

Four

The Resort Idea

Camp Abbot was in operation for only 14 months. Shortly after the war ended, Prineville-based Hudspeth Land and Livestock company purchased the surplus Army property to use for cattle ranching. The property contained 5,484 deeded acres and another 1,031 leased acres and was worth $750,000.

An internal document from the late 1950s shows that the Hudspeth company clearly understood the value of the property beyond traditional farming use:

> Aside from the income to be derived from a 1,000 head cattle operation, the recreational potential must be considered as having the greatest interest for a buyer. Recreational opportunities include hunting, fishing and snow sports. . . . Fishing is excellent on the famous Deschutes River. Snow sports are enjoyed at the multi-million dollar Bachelor Butte Ski Bowl. The highest use of this area would seem to be a resort type subdivision. The existing lodge [Camp Abbot's Officers' Mess] could be a focal point for the entire subdivision.

The development of Sunriver can be attributed to California businessman Lee Evans, Portland attorney Donald McCallum, and Omark Industries founder John Gray.

Evans's involvement in Sunriver came by way of marrying into the Hudspeth family. The Prineville-based company was in dire financial straits, and Evans received a power of attorney to sell the Sunriver land. In an interview in *The Bulletin* in September 1988, Evans said, "The crown jewel of the Hudspeth holdings was what is now Sunriver."

After John Hudspeth defaulted on a loan, which was secured by the former Camp Abbot site, Evans and his wife purchased the property in 1964. With full control over the property, Evans hired Guillermo Lehmann, a Berkeley, California, planner, to develop plans for a resort community to be called Castellaras. The plans called for "dense housing development, a network of waterways, and a golf course"—Central Oregon's version of Venice.

When the US Army left Camp Abbot, most of the buildings were either sold as surplus or razed. The former Camp Abbot officers' mess was the only building left standing, although this picture shows the original officers' mess intact. The lodge-style building, on which so many soldiers worked so hard during their time at Camp Abbot, was left in disrepair. For several years, Bend's baseball team, the Bend Elks, used the building for their summer training camps. The building was later used as hay storage, and some of Hudspeth Land and Livestock Company's 1,000 head of cattle sought shelter from the weather there. Eventually, the building was left unattended. (Both, courtesy of DHM.)

The US Army left a significant amount of infrastructure behind. Hudspeth's inventory listed the following improvements to the area: "high quality roads, bridges and other improvements including a magnificent lodge." Also included on the property were a sewage treatment plant, a barn, a canal, and outbuildings. Decades later, when the Sunriver Owners Association prepared the site to build a new swimming pool, construction crews unearthed wooden water pipes from Camp Abbot. (Courtesy of DHM.)

Hudspeth Land and Livestock Company formed Recreation Unlimited in 1958 to "make active and efficient use" of the land and, admittedly, to make a profit. According to the Hudspeth company, recreation was considered a "land resource." Their land holdings, estimated at 350,000 acres, were opened to anyone willing to pay an annual fee of $35 to enjoy recreation on private land. The former Camp Abbot area was included in Recreation Unlimited offerings. (Courtesy of DHM.)

An avid outdoorsman, Portland real estate lawyer Don McCallum was familiar with Central Oregon and the former Camp Abbot site, having hunted and fished in the area for many years. One of the original investors and eventually co-owner of Sunriver Properties, he and Lee Evans presented the basic outline for Sunriver to John Gray. (Courtesy of DHM.)

John Gray grew up in Monroe, Oregon. After he served in the US Army 82nd Airborne Division during World War II, he became assistant general manager for Oregon Saw Chain Manufacturing Company in 1948. Only six short years later, he bought out the company. Already a well-known resort community developer, Gray followed the success of his development of Salishan on the Oregon coast with Sunriver Resort.

California businessman Lee Evans married Goldie Hudspeth in 1935. Charged with selling the former Camp Abbot site for the Hudspeth Land and Livestock company, Evans developed several proposals to build a resort community on the property. Before Evans saw his vision for a resort community take fruition, he sold his interests in the company to Gray in 1968 to focus on his California businesses. (Courtesy of DHM.)

The last part of the puzzle to develop Sunriver was the hiring of naturalist Jim Anderson (left) and award-winning landscape architect Bob Royston (right). Together with Gray and McCallum, the team submitted master plans for the new community in 1965, and the construction of Sunriver got under way in 1968.

The development of Sunriver was not without its challenges. In May 1972, McCallum filed suit against Gray and demanded Sunriver Properties be sold and its remaining assets distributed to the company's two stockholders. McCallum, a minority stockholder and former president of the company, alleged Gray had "misapplied and wasted Sunriver assets." McCallum alleged Gray had breached an agreement among the three owners, amending the bylaws to allow more shares to be issued, which in turn diluted McCallum's share of the company. At the time, a Deschutes County appraisal valued the Sunriver property at $5.8 million. A year later, McCallum withdrew the suit. The case eventually went to the Oregon Supreme Court, which in 1975 found in favor of Gray. (Above, author's collection; below, courtesy of DHM.)

Five

SUNRIVER TAKES SHAPE

Development of Sunriver was in part driven by a national phenomenon, the so-called "second home boom," which called for an alternative to both big city and rural living. Sunriver's residents would enjoy "privacy, dignity and graceful living," according to a March 1969 article in *The Bulletin*.

When the development of Sunriver was announced to the public in late 1965, the officials of Sunriver Properties envisioned a community of 12,000 to 15,000 people. In an interview with *The Bulletin* in March 1966, general manager Allen Grant said, "We will appeal to active retired people, those from the Willamette Valley who want homes in their area to use part of the year, and to out-of-state people who simply want to get away from the smog and crowds."

He added, "This development will be a 10 to 15 year program and won't be accomplished overnight."

The preliminary plans included a lodge, an 18-hole golf course, service shops, and a small boat basin. The project also included infrastructure such as paved streets, a sewer system, and underground utilities.

Each village cluster would have a character of its own and was planned to house about 5,000 people. In between the villages, large natural areas would provide space for Sunriver residents to enjoy the natural beauty of the area. Connecting the community would be a network of pathways for walking, biking, and riding electric carts.

The developers had grand plans for Sunriver, hoping the community would turn into one of the largest residential recreation areas in the United States.

With great fanfare, Sunriver Lodge was opened to the public in late September 1969. After 10 months of construction and a $1.5 million price tag, the lodge featured a coffee shop, dining area, lounge, kitchen, conference center, banquet rooms, and 77 privately owned condominiums accommodating up to 400 people. Included in the project was the restoration of the former Camp Abbot officers' mess, renamed Sunriver Center.

Construction of Sunriver Lodge got under way in mid-August 1968. This picture shows workers building the concrete forms for the foundation. Between the wood forms, one of the two bridges leading to the south golf course is visible. (Courtesy of DHM.)

Construction of the main resort development continued for almost a full year. Sunriver Lodge, the lodge condominiums, and South Pool stood ready in 1969. The first lots in Meadow Village sold for $7,500. The former Camp Abbot officers' mess is visible to the upper right of the lodge. (Courtesy of Sunriver Resort.)

Built by Vik Construction, Sunriver Lodge opened for business in the fall of 1969. Before the official premiere, the public was invited for an informal ceremony. The event was attended by 100 representatives from the media as well as 300–400 members of the business community and civic leaders. Dick Noble, general manager of the lodge, hoped it would become the convention center of Oregon. (Author's collection.)

The lodge was built featuring Northwest or Cascadian style architecture. Visitors were greeted by dark wood paneling, dark carpets, and exposed wood trusses, which created an intimate feeling. The expansive lobby had large skylights, which added ample light to the interior of the building, and large windows in the restaurant gave visitors an unobstructed view of the Cascade Range. (Courtesy of DHM.)

Construction of Sunriver was big news for the local newspaper. *The Bulletin* photographer followed Don McCallum, president of Sunriver Properties, to the Deschutes County building department in Bend when he presented the master plans for Meadow Village. From left to right are Helen Dacey, county clerk; Dean Seager, vice president of Sunriver; and Don McCallum, president of Sunriver Properties. (Courtesy of DHM.)

After turning in the master plans, all that was left was the official signature from the Deschutes County Commissioners. From left to right are Dorothy Smead, county commissioner; DeVere L. Penhollow, Deschutes County judge; and Gerald "Jerry" McCann, county commissioner. (Courtesy of DHM.)

With the construction of Sunriver Lodge under way, the developers started building the first clusters of cabins and houses in Sunriver. Meadow Village was the first out, followed by the Pole Houses and Cluster Cabins in rapid succession. Individuals also began snapping up lots in the resort community. The first homesite was sold on June 28, 1968. By the end of the year, there were 113 condos and 3 homes in Sunriver.

A mid-August 1968 editorial in *The Bulletin* asked, "Can a top-flight, expensive real estate development succeed in Central Oregon?" The writer posed the question: were Oregonians ready to "pay prices in the Southern California range for top-drawer developments?" According to the editorial, the answer was "yes:" "The Sunriver development on the Deschutes south of Bend seems to be a success." (Courtesy of DHM.)

A special insert in *The Bulletin* on August 23, 1968, extolled the virtues of the new development, telling the readers "Sunriver has a neat, attractive appearance." The former Camp Abbot officers' mess was turned into a sales office for Sunriver Properties. Prospective buyers could visualize the development through scale models of the first two housing developments in Sunriver, Meadow Village and Skypark Village. The wall displays told not only the story of the future of Sunriver, but also what had come before. In the corner, a display showcased the Fort Rock sandals, Henry Larcom Abbot, and Camp Abbot. (Both, courtesy of DHM.)

Real estate sales at Sunriver were brisk in the initial stages of the development. By August 1968, Sunriver Properties recorded 106 real estate transactions that totaled in excess of $2 million. By 1971, the small community had grown to 109 residents. (Courtesy of DHM.)

The developers took great care finding material to enhance the overall look of the sales office, housed in a wing of the old officers' mess. Lumber for the offices was provided by the Miller Lumber Company of Bend, and Doug Remmick of Northwest Stone in Portland, Oregon, was contracted for all the stonework. The highlight was the entrance, which featured green mottled slate from Vermont. (Courtesy of DHM.)

Aside from the construction of a condominium complex close to Sunriver Lodge, the development of Meadow Village was the first in a series of resort living areas built in Sunriver. Prospective homeowners could snap up a cluster cabin starting at $16,000. One of the selling points of the Meadow Village homes was the fact that all utility lines were buried underground. (Courtesy of DHM.)

Another part of the development of Sunriver was the construction of 21 condominium buildings that housed 76 apartments. The model units featured furnishings and appliances "from all over the world," according to a special insert in *The Bulletin*. "Owners will enjoy the comfort, convenience and privacy of smartly designed, well-constructed, handsomely furnished apartments." Another feature of Sunriver homeownership was the opportunity to rent out the condos to vacationers. (Courtesy of DHM.)

Sunriver was first and foremost about recreation. The expanse that is the Great Meadow—once historic Lake Benham where Native Americans camped around the shores, and thousands of years later, soldiers from Camp Abbot trained—now featured different kinds of activities. Sunriver Lodge, the crown jewel in the development, was supported by recreational facilities nearby. The future south golf course is visible in the center and to the left of the lodge. (Courtesy of DHM.)

The first nine holes of the south course were developed in conjunction with the construction of the lodge and other resort infrastructure. Designed by Lake Oswego, Oregon, course designer Fred Federspiel, the back nine of the planned 18-hole south course opened in 1969. The front nine was ready a year later. The south course was later renamed The Meadows at Sunriver with additional design by John Fought in 1999. (Courtesy of DHM.)

John Gray had already worked with Federspiel, who designed the course at Salishan Resort. Before they met, Federspiel had designed several other courses in Oregon and Washington, among them Royal Oak in the early 1950s and Pineway Golf Course in 1958. (Courtesy of DHM.)

Maintaining a green and cool golf course during the warm and dry Central Oregon summer months takes a lot of water. A local Bend firm, Inglis Pump and Welding, installed the irrigation system for the course, while Portland company Baltz and Sons laid down the pipes and sprinklers for the system. (Courtesy of DHM.)

After the golf course was finished, Sunriver's maintenance staff took over the responsibilities for its upkeep. The man in charge of the golf course was Joe Ward. Sunriver had a large fleet of maintenance vehicles. This one is parked at the platted golf course across Sun River, with the Great Hall in the background. (Courtesy of DHM.)

Originally conceived as a convenience to the developers who had to travel to and from Portland, the Sunriver Airport runway was constructed almost immediately following the start of the lodge project. At a cost of $197,000, Sunriver was equipped with a paved airstrip from day one. It was a stroke of genius that had potential out-of-area home buyers taking notice. (Courtesy of DHM.)

The move to build an airstrip attracted well-to-do clients to Sunriver. The airport featured a small office with communication capabilities between the airport and incoming airplanes, as well as refueling facilities. Sunriver Airport was inaugurated on August 11, 1968, with a "fly-in" from the Hillsboro chapter of the Oregon Pilot's Association. (Courtesy of DHM.)

After almost 25 years of neglect, Col. Frank Besson's "training project," the Camp Abbot officers' mess, was lovingly restored to its former glory. When Camp Abbot veteran John Banks, who designed the lodge-style building, returned to Sunriver in 1989, he said, "it looks better now than when we finished it." (Courtesy of DHM.)

The former officers' mess building quickly became a focal point of the sales efforts. Referred to as Sunriver Center, the log building housed sales and administrative offices, a small cafeteria for prospective buyers, and a large outdoor archway to soak in the summer sun. The officers of Sunriver Properties Inc. used the structure, which later became known as the Great Hall, as a gathering place for official functions. (Courtesy of DHM.)

The Sunriver project was initially seen as a threat to Bend businesses, who saw the resort community as a potential competitor for local business. To calm frazzled nerves, developer John Gray invited Bend Chamber of Commerce members to a forum at the Sunriver Center in April 1969. With no restaurant facilities in operation, the visiting members were served box lunches at the meeting. (Courtesy of DHM.)

Addressing 130 chamber members, Gray made it "abundantly clear that Sunriver intends to maintain friendly relations with its neighbors in Central Oregon." He emphasized that the development of Sunriver would have a far-reaching impact on the region, well beyond the geographical limits of the resort community. Seen here is a scale model of Meadow Village. (Courtesy of DHM.)

Gray emphasized to the chamber members that Sunriver supported the local economy. Up to that date, he estimated, the developers had spent $4 million on building Sunriver, with much more to come during the 20 to 30 years it would take for full development. At the time of his presentation, 48 people were already on the permanent payroll, and the ongoing construction projects employed another 178. (Courtesy of DHM.)

The gathering served its purpose, and the Bend Chamber of Commerce decided the development held promise for both Sunriver and Bend. An editorial in *The Bulletin* the day after the presentation noted, "Central Oregon has an important stake in the success of Sunriver. The friendly hand extended by John Gray should assure a continued spirit of mutual respect and cooperation." (Courtesy of DHM.)

In 1977, Sunriver Properties Inc. proposed to sell 3,400 undeveloped acres to the US government for addition to the Deschutes National Forest. Federal law prohibited the sale of private land to the US government without approval from the county government. Deschutes County commissioners worried the sale would affect the county's bottom line. Commissioner Bob Montgomery told *The Bulletin* in February 1977 that "there is less and less privately-owned land which can be included on county tax rolls, and a sale to the Forest Service would decrease that further." In September 1977, Sunriver Properties and the US Forest Service signed a letter of intent for the sale of 3,187 acres. The commissioners nixed the sale at their October 5, 1977, hearing. A year later, the commissioners finally approved the sale of 2,185 acres to the US Forest Service. The sale was completed in October 1978 and brought in a much-needed cash infusion of $2.8 million, which helped secure future development of Sunriver. From left to right are unidentified, forest supervisor Earl Nichols, Deschutes National Forest and Land Adjustment status and claims officer Carlin Jackson of the Forest Service's Pacific Northwest Regional office in Portland, and the Forest Service's Kay Coyner taking notes. (Courtesy of DHM.)

Six

Building a Modern City

As the resort and residential community of Sunriver grew, the need for fire protection, law enforcement, and public works services had to be met by the developers. Sunriver Resort established the Sunriver Fire Department in 1968. Housed in a small cabin across the road from today's Village at Sunriver, the fire department's first fire chief was Herbert "Junior" Kappel, who held the position until 1976.

The volunteer firefighters received basic firefighting training from the members of the City of Bend Fire Department. The first major incident Sunriver's firefighters faced was the "Big Fire" of 1970, when two buildings, containing eight condominiums, caught fire. The volunteer fire fighters battled the blaze.

Originally a part of Sunriver Resort, ownership of the Sunriver Fire Department was transferred to the SROA in the late 1980s. Although privately owned and operated, the Sunriver Fire Department operated as if it were a public entity. It was dispatched by the Deschutes County 911 and had mutual assistance agreements with the City of Bend Fire Department, the La Pine Rural Fire Protection District, and the US Forest Service. More recently, the fire department became a public entity as a component of a tax-supported public service district.

The Sunriver Police Department began as a volunteer police force in the 1970s. Originally called the Sunriver Department of Public Safety, the volunteer officers had little authority or equipment to do their job effectively. After serving with the Washington State Patrol, Paul Peterson decided to move to Sunriver. Not ready to retire, he became Sunriver chief of police in September 1988. Today, the police department is part of the tax-supported service district.

The Public Works Department was established by Sunriver Properties and was eventually turned over to the Sunriver Owners Association. The headquarters for the director of public works was originally housed in leftover Camp Abbot buildings, which were used for office space, mechanic shops, and storage for road equipment. In 1990, the department moved into a new building, but one of the former US Army sewage treatment roundhouses is still used as a maintenance building.

Sunriver's first fire engine was a brand-new Western States pumper, followed by a 1945 American LaFrance purchased from the San Jose, California, fire department in 1970. The LaFrance was replaced by a new Seagrave structural fire engine (pictured). The department grew by leaps and bounds throughout the 1970s and 1980s. In August 1984, the department purchased a used 1954 sixty-five-foot ladder truck from the Portland Fire Department. (Courtesy of Sunriver Fire Department.)

As firefighting technology evolved, outdated equipment was replaced with more modern fire apparatus. In 1990, the department replaced the ladder truck with a modern 50-foot "Telesquirt" fire truck.

The first fire station was housed in an old cabin that contained an office and a firefighter bunkroom. The building was located across Abbot Drive from Sunriver Village from 1988 to 1996. The fire apparatus and ambulance were housed in a warehouse across the parking lot from the cabin.

The foundation of Sunriver Fire Department was built on a devoted group of volunteer firefighters. The first firefighters were trained by members of the Bend Fire Department. The first major fire in Sunriver happened in late April 1970, when eight condominiums were lost to a rapidly moving fire. Personnel from both Sunriver and La Pine Fire Departments battled the fire for five hours.

Sunriver Fire Department eventually outgrew its cramped quarters, and in 1995 the SROA approved the construction of a new 12,577-square-foot fire station. The new $914,000 building was inaugurated on January 14, 1995. Sunriver's fire station features a dormitory for the department's fire and EMS personnel, four bays to house the department's fire apparatus and ambulance, and a tower for hanging and drying fire hoses. Above, from left to right, Fire Chief Scott Alvord, Capt. Shannon Brownlee, fire medic Cathy Smith, and Assistant Fire Chief Larry Long are pictured in front of the new fire station. Pictured below at the 9/11 memorial celebration in 2002 are Fire Chief Pat McGinnis (far left) and interim fire chief Rod Bjorvik (right of the flagpole).

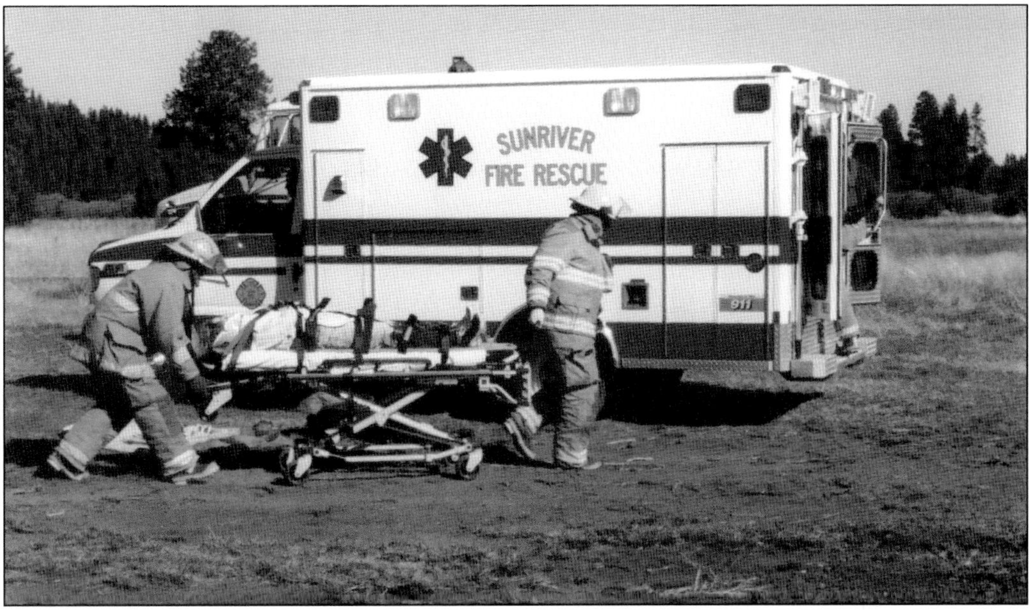

Approximately four years after the founding of the Sunriver Fire Department, the department absorbed Sunriver Emergency Medical Service. In 1972, the combined department purchased a 1958 Ford station wagon to function as a medical response vehicle. Over the decades, the department has operated increasingly modern ambulances.

The Sunriver Fire Department struts its stuff at the annual Fourth of July picnic held in Sunriver's spacious Fort Rock Park. From the early volunteer fire department to today's fully staffed fire station with modern fire apparatus and ambulance, the community is well served by its own fire and rescue services.

A predecessor to the Sunriver Police Department, the Department of Public Safety policed the community for many years. To augment the threadbare resources during the formative years of Sunriver, the community instituted a volunteer-based Citizen Patrol neighborhood watch group. Here is Chief J.R. Elliot with the Department of Public Safety outside his office in October 1986.

Chief Pete Wanless (center) is pictured in front of the police station when it was located in Building 13 in The Village at Sunriver, offices the Sunriver Music Festival occupies today. Behind the chief are volunteers from the community's Citizen Patrol.

As the police department started formalizing its organization, it became clear that state laws did not recognize Sunriver's city charter. The staff was paid and hired by SROA, but to become eligible to make arrests and write speeding tickets, Sunriver's rural police department had to be organized and trained under the supervision of the Deschutes County Sheriff's Office.

Sunriver Police Department officers employ modern technology to enforce laws and regulations. Here, an officer uses radar to detect speeding drivers on community roadways.

In 2001, Deschutes County Sheriff Les Stiles (right) began the process of having his office accredited by the Oregon Association of Chiefs of Police. That required Sheriff Stiles to exert more oversight of the Sunriver Police Department—the officers of which were deputized by his office—or decommission the department, which would lose the authority to detain or arrest people committing crimes or traffic offenses. That announcement jarred Police Chief Mike Kennedy (left) as well as the entire community of Sunriver, who just weeks earlier had voted down creating a tax district for the police and fire departments. At the time, Sunriver property owners paid a monthly $67 maintenance fee, of which $31 went to funding the police and fire departments, raising approximately $2.4 million a year. The SROA again put the issue to a vote. In May 2002, faced with the potential loss of their police department, SROA members voted to form a tax-supported service district. The new taxing district went into effect in November 2002, and funds police and fire services through property taxes.

With the taxing district in place, the Sunriver Police Department operates as any city law enforcement organization. Although major crimes are few and far between, property crimes, drug busts, and speeding drivers keep the police force busy. This 15-mile-long high-speed pursuit—70 miles per hour on Cottonwood Road—ended with a slip off the road on Circle 6 after the driver lost control of the stolen vehicle.

Slick winter roads also keep Sunriver's police force busy throughout the winter season. Perched at 4,100 feet, Sunriver is prone to large amounts of snow. Although the SROA Public Works Department is out in an instant to keep the roads clear, visitors and residents alike can experience a 360-degree spin on the icy roads.

The Sunriver Public Works Department is responsible for the year-round maintenance of the community's more than 60 miles of roads and more than 30 miles of pathways, as well as street signs and lights. The staff also maintains SROA-owned facilities such as the Sunriver Homeowners Aquatic & Recreation Center, the North Pool, and tennis facilities. Originally housed in the remnants of Camp Abbot's sewer sedimentation tanks, the public works building was described as "the worst building facility in Sunriver" in the 2012 Infrastructure and Amenities Master Plan.

The old Corporation Yard is also home to the community's recycling center. A portion of the yard is also used to store owners' RVs and boats during the winter months. One of Camp Abbot's sewer treatment buildings finally was deemed unsafe for use and was turned into a cinder bin for winter road maintenance.

The Sunriver Public Works Department moved into a brand new building in 2000. With modern offices and repair facilities, the new building is a huge step up from the Camp Abbot roundhouses. In a 2012 land swap with Sunriver Resort, the public works department gained access to an additional two acres for future development. The department is home to 14 employees.

SROA fleet service performs contract work on Sunriver fire and police department vehicles as well as emergency/fire vehicles from the La Pine Rural Fire Protection District. Dan McLaughlin is one of three mechanics working for SROA's Public Works Department. He was hired in 2006 and holds 11 certifications that allow him to work on ambulances and fire trucks.

Nature has a way of making life interesting, especially for the Public Works Department. The winter of 1992–1993 was one for the record books. Throughout the season, Sunriver received 144 inches of snow, a record almost broken during the winter of 2016–2017, locally known as "Snowmageddon." Sunriver's street maintenance personnel were out in full force, clearing more than 60 miles of roads and over 30 miles of paths. The snow chaos also created a headache for homeowners who had to deal with heavy snow loads on their roofs and the threat of ice damming, not to mention shoveling snow off their driveway only to have snowbanks thrown up when snowplows came through. The front-page headline of the January 1993 *Sunriver Scene* says it all: "Who Put the Snow in My Driveway?"

Skiing has a long tradition in Central Oregon. Scandinavian mill workers founded Bend's ski club, the Skyliners, in 1927. When Bill Healey, a former World War II 10th Mountain Division veteran, set out to develop a Central Oregon ski area, Skyliners pointed to Bachelor Butte as the best option. At first, access to Mount Bachelor from Sunriver was via Bend—a 38-mile round-trip. To promote Sunriver as a winter destination resort community, Sunriver Resort obtained a special-use permit from the US Forest Service in July 1983 to convert an unimproved Forest Service logging road into a year-around access road to Mount Bachelor. Inaugurated on November 17, 1983, to great fanfare, Mount Bachelor president Bill Healey rode in the lead car on the first drive to the ski resort. Following Spring River Road (Forest Service Road 40) and a new stretch (Forest Service Road 46), the $800,000 construction cost was paid in its entirety by Sunriver Resort. The new 11.5-mile road was a blessing for skiers and snowboarders, as it drastically cut down drive time to Mount Bachelor.

In 2000, the SROA moved from its offices in the Village Mall to a newly built administration building in the same area as the fire station. The building also houses the Sunriver Police Department.

Sunriver is home to a dedicated group of residents. Members of the close-knit community of about 1,000 are deeply involved in how the area is run. The annual homeowner meetings are attended in great numbers, and if there are issues of interest to the entire community, the SROA calls for public meetings. The local newspaper, the *Sunriver Scene*, covers the meetings in detail and highlights news from SROA board meetings. The newspaper also has a standing column written by SROA's president.

As Rosalind says in Shakespeare's *As You Like It*, "good wine needs no bush." Since 1987, The Village at Sunriver has been the scene of an annual wine festival. The purpose of the event was to pair local wines with discerning palates. Over the years, the festival honoring Northwest wine and good conversations has grown rapidly, featuring over 40 vendors. Today, it is known as Uncorked, and is held at the Sunriver Homeowners Aquatic & Recreation Center (SHARC).

Warm weather and a swimming pool go well together. The construction of the South Pool in front of Sunriver Lodge was a clear indication the developers had the right idea how to cool off during hot Central Oregon summers. When the 40-year-old pool showed signs of wear and tear, Sunriver's homeowners decided it was time to plan for the next 40 years with a brand new recreation and aquatic center.

The SROA maintains 24 tennis and 6 pickleball courts throughout the community. Tennis promotes a healthy lifestyle, one of the hallmarks of Sunriver. Homeowners also stay active playing pickleball. Originally a children's backyard pastime, pickleball is a mix of tennis, badminton, and ping-pong. Founded in 2012, Sunriver's Pickleball Club has dedicated courts at Fort Rock Park.

Sunriver provides much more than just activities for grown-ups. Kids of all ages, residents and visitors alike, are presented with a dizzying array of choices.

Sunriver Preparatory School was the community's first school. Founded in 1983, the private school taught students from Kindergarten through 12th grade. During its first year in operation, Sunriver Prep had 65 students, which doubled the following year, leading to a quick classroom expansion. In addition to teaching basic curriculum, the for-profit school put an emphasis on offering advanced classes in math, language, art, and drama. Later, Sunriver Prep left Sunriver and moved closer to Bend.

Three Rivers Elementary School opened for the 1989–1990 school year with three modular units covering kindergarten to first grade. The next two school years, the Three Rivers School expanded with classes for third grade, and then fourth and fifth grades. At the same time, the school grew to nine modular units in the Sunriver Business Park.

By the 2003–2004 school year, Three Rivers School taught students through the eighth grade thanks to a 25,000-square-foot addition, which included new classrooms. In 2006, voters approved a construction bond for the Bend La Pine School District. As a result, a $7.3 million middle school wing solved Three Rivers School's overcrowding issues. The new wing separated elementary and middle school students.

Three Rivers School students have busy schedules. Teachers and staff strive to provide a world-class education that meets each student's individual needs. The Sunriver Music Festival and Three Rivers School have, over the years, combined resources in the form of music workshops for students. Conducted by artists normally connected with the music festival's Fireside Program, the students get a chance to experience classical, jazz, and world music through the workshops.

Sunriver Library is a vital part of the Deschutes Public Library. Dreamed up by a group of enthusiasts in 1995, the Friends of Sunriver Library worked hard over the next three years to overcome seemingly overwhelming goals. Funding, location, and design were top priorities. The initial group included George Riser, called "the father of Sunriver library," and Barbara Wade, "mother" of the library, along with Monet Beith, Bill McCann, Nancy Ruel, and Shirley Walton. After a phone survey among voters in the three taxing districts indicated they were willing to fund a library through a bond measure, the project came to fruition in 1998. Today, the 6,800-square-foot building houses a large collection of books, music, and DVDs for adults, teens, and children. The airy design includes a public meeting room and a cozy fireplace.

Seven

Nature Takes Center Stage

Sunriver emphasizes care for the environment. A tradition of focusing equal treatment on the development of Sunriver while preserving its natural landscape was established early in the history of the community. John Gray had already shown concerns for the environment as he developed Salishan Resort on the Oregon Coast. Compared with the Salishan project, Sunriver was almost 10 times larger. Gray's vision for Sunriver was "to create a commercial enterprise that blends into the environment without insult."

By chance, Gray encountered Jim Anderson. At the time, Anderson was teaching outdoor school for Oregon Museum of Science and Industry in Portland, and one of Gray's children attended one of his classes. Anderson was hired as Sunriver's first naturalist. Gray also hired award-winning landscape architect Robert Royston.

Rayston and Anderson were the perfect match for the development of Sunriver. Before their arrival, the plan was simply to subdivide the area and sell individual lots. It was hardly an approach that would have taken Sunriver to where it is today. Encouraged by Royston and Anderson, Gray committed to new plans for a residential community with a strong environmental focus.

Anderson had three major responsibilities. He acted as an environmental consultant to the land developer, ran outdoor recreation programs for Sunriver residents and guests, and had environmental oversight of the community.

Sunriver Properties provided Anderson with an office and space to run his outdoor activities. Named the Ecologium, it was housed in the Abbot House. In 1974–1975, the Ecologium moved into a building off Circle One, today occupied by Sunriver's Human Resource Department. By this time, Anderson had left his position, and in late 1972, Jay Bowerman took over.

In 1982, Sunriver Properties donated eight acres of land near Lake Aspen for a permanent nature center building. The spot, originally picked by Anderson and Royston, became the new headquarters in 1984. In 1991, an observatory was constructed next door, eventually creating the Sunriver Nature Center and Observatory.

Jim Anderson grew up near West Haven, Connecticut. Moving to Bend in 1951, Anderson got a job with the US Forest Service fighting wildland fires. He ended up staying in Oregon, although his grandfather thought he was "nuts." For a while, Anderson served as a naturalist for the Oregon Museum of Science and Industry. While there, he was introduced to John Gray and eventually became one of his first employees.

Jay Bowerman is the current manager of Sunriver Nature Center. With a master's degree in biology from the University of Oregon, Bowerman wanted to become a teacher. He was working as a substitute teacher in the Bend La Pine School District when he got a full-time job as the resident naturalist in Sunriver. For more than 30 years, Bowerman has been the guiding spirit of the Sunriver Nature Center and remains the institution's principal researcher. (Photograph by Les Joslin.)

The Sunriver Nature Center is the most obvious manifestation of the developer's pledge to strike a balance between commercial necessity and environmental concerns. Since its inception, the Nature Center has kept up with its original mission of "inspiring present and future generations to cherish and understand our natural world." (Courtesy of Sunriver Nature Center.)

The Sunriver Nature Center added another dimension with the construction of the observatory next door, a favorite among both kids and adults. Compared with many communities in Central Oregon, Sunriver offers a relatively dark night sky, which is a must for serious stargazing.

Open year-round, the Nature Center has two distinct seasons. During the school year, it offers field trips to local schools and outreach programs to kindergarten through fifth-grade classes. The Nature Center's "traveling trunk" program is successful in classroom settings throughout Central Oregon. When the school year wraps up in June, the Nature Center becomes a gathering place for inquisitive Sunriver homeowners and tourists.

The commitment to uphold the Nature Center's mission takes staff and a dedicated group of more than 170 volunteers. Money to run the Nature Center comes from memberships, programs, donations, grants, and contracts with the Sunriver Resort and the SROA. The other half of the operating budget comes from the Second Tern Thrift Shop located on Spring River Road. Pictured is former Sunriver Nature Center manager Jennifer Curtis with young volunteers.

Lake Aspen was home to Chuck and Grace, two trumpeter swans inhabiting the lake since 2013, part of a breeding program to reintroduce trumpeter swans in the area. During the breeding season, Chuck was known to protect Grace and their offspring from wild geese and humans. Unable to fly but free to roam the area, Chuck was illegally killed downstream from Lake Aspen by a hunter on Thanksgiving 2017.

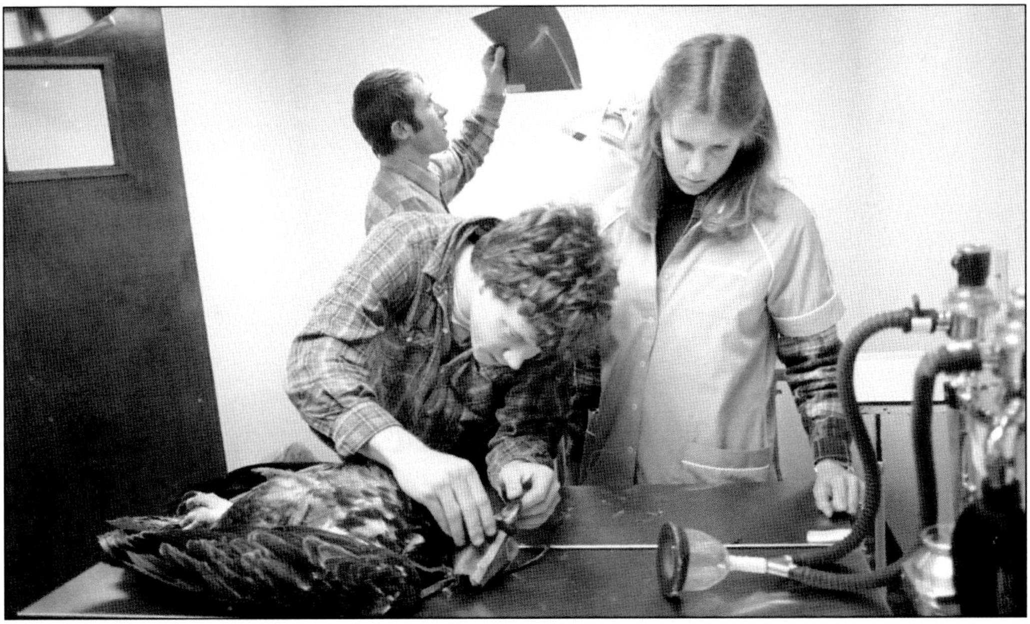

Sunriver Nature Center once had its own rehabilitation center to care for wounded raptors brought in by Oregon State Police or Sunriver residents. This female golden eagle was found with a gunshot wound to her wing. Here, future veterinarian Jeff Cooney and veterinarian Holly Harned remove bullet fragments and feathers while Jay Bowerman checks out an X-ray. Eventually, the eagle ended up in a breeding program. (Courtesy of DHM.)

Sunriver Nature Center's bird and animal rehabilitation efforts have enjoyed success over the years. This eight-month-old great horned owl suffered head trauma when it was hit by a car near Pilot Butte in Bend. After spending six weeks recuperating at the Nature Center, the owl was released. Here, Jay Bowerman and vet tech Marnie Brown with the Sunriver Vet Clinic return the owl to the wild.

Sunriver Nature Center has taken a keen interest in the frogs and toads living in Lake Aspen. Every spring, the toads migrate from the lake into nearby forest land, which puts them in danger of being run over by bikes or cars. During hectic weeks, Sunriver residents pluck the migrating toads from the roads and pathways and send them off to the safer environment on the other side of the asphalt paths.

Another threat to the frog population is the bullfrog. Giant-sized compared to the native frogs, the bullfrog eats everything in its way. The ongoing bullfrog eradication program has proved tough. The population of the non-native species has exploded during the last 10 years. Between 2008 and 2014, approximately 40–140 were removed each year. During the summer of 2017, the SROA removal program netted more than 5,000 bullfrogs.

The Oregon Observatory at Sunriver is the community's best kept secret. Next door to Sunriver Nature Center, the observatory has the largest collection of telescopes for public use in the country. The top of the line is a 30-inch Newtonian telescope, donated by the Matthews family in 2012. Originally housed in the Glass Starport, it got a home of its own in 2013 when the observatory constructed the Karen Clark Star Deck, a roll-off building. Other telescopes include a 20-inch StarMaster Newtonian, a 20-inch Ritchey-Chretien, and a JMI NGT 12.5-inch donated by the Sunriver Rotary Club in 2016. (Both, courtesy of Tracy Benton Brown via the *Sunriver Scene*.)

It is not often kids are allowed to look at the sun. Moms and dads always say, "no way." But when the kids come to the Oregon Observatory in Sunriver for a daytime visit, anything goes. Thanks to specially filtered telescopes, kids and adults alike can get a view of sunspots and other solar features. Future astronauts can also take part in rocket classes at the Sunriver Nature Center

The observatory also offers After Hours Deep Field Exploration programs for hardcore astronomy enthusiasts. "Night owls" arrive at the observatory at 11:00 p.m. and stay until 1:00 a.m. When the roof rolls off the main telescopes, the night sky opens up for a closer look at faraway galaxies. Due to its 4,164-foot elevation, Sunriver's dark and clear skies offer a view of billions of stars.

Homeowner interaction with Sunriver's other residents is quite common. The staff at Sunriver Nature Center often field questions from curious homeowners who come in direct contact with elk, deer, owls, the occasional bear, and other wildlife. They want to know what to do about the coyote with a limp walking through their yard or the seemingly abandoned fawn (do nothing), or how to deal with squirrels pulling insulation out of their crawl space, raccoons living underneath their hot tub, or bats roosting over their front door. The staff also help homeowners with suggestions about what kind of native plant species can be planted to enhance the natural landscaping. The owlets above decided to hang out on a deck to catch some sun, while the herd of elk below enjoy lunchtime on a fairway.

The Deschutes River snakes through Sunriver for more than five miles on its way from the Cascades to the Columbia River. Prior to logging by Bend sawmills, much of the river was lined by big ponderosa and lodgepole pines. The trees prevented bank erosion, and when they died and fell into the river, they added habitat for the many species of trout that populate the area. To protect river banks and improve breeding grounds, the SROA Natural Resources Department, in partnership with the Oregon Department of Fish and Wildlife, conducts an ongoing river restoration program. Among its efforts is to bring the river back to its historic past by placing dead trees along the banks and revegetating the fragile strip of land between the walking paths and the river. The Sunriver Anglers Club is also an active partner in the projects.

Sunriver's developers' commitment to creating an ecologically sustainable community is manifested in Sunriver being one of the first privately owned communities in Oregon to be recognized as a Tree City USA by the Arbor Day Foundation. Sunriver has successfully maintained the designation since 1980.

Every spring, students from Three Rivers School and volunteers plant ponderosa pine seedlings throughout the community. The area was heavily logged during the heyday of the Bend sawmills. Project Ponderosa was started in 2006 by Sunriver resident and retired teacher Lee Stevenson. Known as "Tree Man," he found fertile ground with teachers and students at Sunriver area's Three Rivers School. The project aims to reforest sensitive areas around Sunriver and beyond.

Eight

Recreation Unlimited

Sunriver is home to a little over a thousand permanent residents who have chosen to live a comfortable life in a serene part of Central Oregon. The small community also attracts thousands of overnight visitors during the summer and winter months. No matter the activity level, Sunriver features nearly unlimited recreational opportunities.

Summer recreation in Sunriver brings together sun and water, as hinted in the name of the community. The area boasts more than 300 days of sunshine a year, and the SROA and Sunriver Resort make sure residents and visitors have plenty of opportunities to enjoy the beautiful weather—summer and winter alike.

Golf enthusiasts can pick from four courses. Crosswater was named one of America's 100 Greatest Courses by *Golf Digest*. The Woodlands and Meadows courses are other options. Although technically not inside Sunriver proper, golfers can also enjoy the latest area course, family-friendly Caldera Springs. This course was named one of the Top 10 Destinations for Family Golf by *Golf Digest* in 2016.

The brand-new Sunriver Homeowners Aquatic & Recreation Center (SHARC) and The Cove pool complex offer entertainment for adults and kids. Fort Rock Park on the northern end of Sunriver provides hours of entertainment. The park has a huge playground, a sand volleyball court, horseshoe pits, a softball/soccer field, tennis/pickleball courts, and a pavilion with tables and barbeques for rent.

With a world-class ski mountain around the corner, Sunriver is truly a year-round resort community. Only a half-hour drive away, Mount Bachelor is a winter sports enthusiast's dream come true. Founded by World War II 10th Mountain Division veteran Bill Healey in the late 1950s, the resort has plenty of room for downhill action for both boarders and skiers. Located in the middle of the Deschutes National Forest, the resort's nordic center features more than 56 miles of groomed cross-country trails.

Golf has always been a top highlight of the Sunriver lifestyle. One of the first major recreational investments of Sunriver Resort was the south course. Developer John Gray had worked with Eugene, Oregon, course designer Fred Federspiel at Salishan and invited him back to design the Meadows. The practice green is located just off Sunriver Lodge, with the Meadows' first tee slightly to the south. The course meanders along Sunriver, with the ninth hole back at the lodge. If sand traps and water hazards have caused too much trouble at this point, the Twisted River Tavern is a short walk across the bridge. (Above, courtesy of DHM.)

The Meadows course was redesigned in 1999 by legendary Portland course designer John Fought. The par-71 course, at 7,012 yards, is considered a test for even world-class golfers. A 2014 review in *The Bulletin* described the course as "more challenging than it appears." The serene landscape, with views overlooking the meadow and Mount Bachelor's snowcapped peak, lulls the golfer into thinking they are in for a relaxing round. But as the reviewer put it, "Make no mistake, though, Meadows is a serious golf course that is a far better test than it appears at first glimpse of the exposed design and generous fairways."

Sunriver offers up four golf courses for the most discerning player. The south course (now the Meadows) was first out, quickly followed by the north course (now Woodlands) in 1981. Designed by Robert Trent Jones Jr., the course received national recognition in 1988 by *Golf* magazine, which ranked the north course No. 21 among America's 75 top courses.

Described as a "challenging resort course," The Woodlands is heavily lined by ponderosa and lodgepole pines. The course meanders through Sunriver's northern interior. The next addition was the Crosswater course, designed by Bob Cupp in 1995. Adjacent to Sunriver, family-friendly nine-hole Caldera Links opened in 2007. Together with the three other Sunriver courses, golfers of all skill levels, like Peter Jacobson (pictured), can find the perfect place to play.

Sunriver played host to the JELD-WEN Traditions golf tournament from 2003 to 2010. Part of the Champions Tour, the tournament attracted world-class golfers to play the Crosswater course just south of Sunriver. Golf fans lined up to watch hall of fame professionals such as Peter Jacobson play. Today, Sunriver Resort is producing the Pacific Amateur Golf Classic (PacAm). The three-day, 54-hole stroke play tournament brings amateur players from all over the world to Sunriver.

One of the first family-friendly recreational opportunities in Sunriver was the swimming pool located just southeast of Sunriver Lodge. Called the South Pool, the five-lane swimming pool was designed by Bend architect Gil Helling.

A favorite summer hangout for visitors and residents alike since 1969, the South Pool started showing the effects of wear and tear. The cracking pool deck was repaired for the 2007 summer season, and the following year, cracks appeared at the bottom of the pool. As the pool neared the end of its life, the SROA and Sunriver Resort in October 2011 discussed a land swap that included the South Pool.

The SROA was already planning for a new recreation complex to replace the aging South Pool. In February 2011, the SROA set out on an ambitious $18.9 million project to turn 22 acres into a combined amphitheater, event center, and pool complex. The new recreation complex was named Sunriver Homeowners Aquatic & Recreation Center, or SHARC, after owners voted in favor of the new name in 2010.

At the February 2011 SHARC groundbreaking, John Salzer, Sunriver resident and chair of the Communications Task Force, told the crowd, "In fact, John Gray, one of Sunriver's founding fathers, always envisioned an amphitheater here." With Sunriver lacking a major recreation facility for almost a year, the frenzied construction continued throughout the summer and fall 2011 with a projected launch in May 2012.

The new aquatic and recreation center stood ready in early 2012. Staff started moving into the new facilities in March 2012, and SHARC was unofficially inaugurated in April when Three Rivers School students, enrolled in the Fun After School Time (FAST) program tried out the pool. The official ribbon-cutting ceremony was held on April 14, 2012. With weather in mind, indoor facilities opened up in late April, and the outdoor pool complex followed a month later.

The new recreation center features indoor and outdoor pools with waterslides, an outdoor adult hot tub, expansive sun-bathing areas, a sand play area, an amphitheater, a winter tubing hill, a summer disc golf course, and an owners-only fitness center. SHARC also rents out space for community gatherings and private events.

Not unlike the pond monkeys of the bygone logging era, kids today can float logs from one side of the pool to the other. The pond monkeys would have appreciated the safety net seen here as they wrestled the logs on the river before sending them up the green chain to be cut. Here, future log rollers, or "birlers," can practice much needed skills of grace and balance.

Sunriver has a long history of environmentally friendly transportation alternatives. The community has over 30 miles of paved pathways, making it possible to leave the car in the garage while walking or biking to the grocery store, golf course, or Sunriver Nature Center. At one time, there were over 100,000 registered bikes in the area including homeowners and bike rental businesses. In the inset is a bike registration sticker.

The popularity of bicycles as mode of transportation has challenged the Sunriver Police Department, which expanded its service with bike patrols cruising the paths throughout the summer months. In 2008, the police department's bike patrol was awarded the Deschutes County Bicycle and Pedestrian Advisory Committee's Big Chainring Award. The award has been given out annually since 1996 to honor individuals, businesses, organizations, and agencies that have made extraordinary efforts to advance bicycling in Deschutes County.

Recreational access to the Deschutes River has been at the top of the list from day one. Today, Sunriver Resort and the SROA provide access points along the river. Floating fashion has changed considerably over the years, from rowboats to kayaks, canoes, inner tubes, stand-up paddle boards, and other floating devices.

There are several public launch and take-out points along the mighty Deschutes River. The Marina is the starting point for many river floating adventures throughout the summer months. River enthusiasts can expect at least two hours of floating time from the Marina to the last takeout before the river takes a rapid plunge north via Benham and Dillon Falls. (Author's collection.)

During the hot Central Oregon summer months, it is not uncommon to see a flotilla of floating devices moving down the Deschutes River. At times, it seems almost possible to walk from one side of the river to the other, jumping from canoe, to kayak, to rubber dinghy without getting wet. Flowing from the high lakes farther upstream, the river is the perfect place to cool down.

After a relaxing trip down the Deschutes River, it is time to take out the floating devices. The river is well-signed for calm-water floaters. This sign points to the next to last point of exit. The last watercraft takeout is at the Benham Falls Day Use Area.

After Lava Butte erupted approximately 6,000 years ago, the lava stream from the small volcano dammed up the river, creating a lake. The water finally found a way out along a narrow gully fronted by lava and forest. The stretch of river between Benham and Dillon Falls is as dangerous as it gets, with sharp lava rocks lurking just below the surface and unpredictable undertow.

Once the river returns to a more manageable state, area river rafting companies are more than happy to give white-water enthusiasts a chance to try out several Class 2 and Class 3 rapids, collectively called the Big Eddy. Under the watchful eyes of certified river guides, locals and tourists alike can opt for a guaranteed wet ride down the safer stretches of the Deschutes River.

Among the many events drawing visitors to Sunriver is the Pacific Crest Endurance Sports Festival in June. Known as the jewel of multisport events in the Northwest, it includes biking, swimming, and running events spread out over three days. The event draws over 5,000 athletes and an additional 10,000 family and friends to Sunriver. Starting on Friday, competitors can pick from 25K and 50K trail runs or Tour de Crest bike tours covering 26 and 55 miles. On Saturday is the long course triathlon, which includes a 1.2-mile swim, 56.3-mile bicycle race, and 13.1-mile run. The marathon on Saturday is a Boston qualifier. Sunday is set aside for an Olympic-distance triathlon (1.5K swim, 28-mile bike course, and a 10K run). (Both, courtesy of Bob Woodward.)

Sen. Bob Packwood of Oregon inaugurated Sunriver's ice-skating rink in 1984. The rink was also intended for roller-skating, but that never took hold in Sunriver. The 26-year-old rink received a much-needed overhaul in 2010 as part of a modernization of The Village at Sunriver. Enhancements included raising the claustrophobia-inducing roof, a warming hut, a remodeled lobby area, and an on-site storage facility for the ice-resurfacing Zamboni. Aside from ice-skating, the rink is also used for men's and youth ice hockey games and coed broomball. In the summer, the facility is turned into a miniature golf course.

Taking cues from members of Bend's pioneering ski club, the Skyliners, Bachelor Butte ski area was developed by Bill Healy in the late 1950s. He decided to take advantage of the "ski fever" that developed shortly after the end of World War II when returning US Army 10th Mountain Division veterans began developing ski resorts in the United States based on concepts they had seen in Europe during the war.

An easy drive from Sunriver, the Mount Bachelor winter sports area on the Deschutes National Forest makes Sunriver a year-round recreation community and destination resort. Mount Bachelor is the largest ski resort in Oregon by area and the second largest single-mountain ski resort in the United States. The resort has over 100 runs covering all levels from novice to expert and is serviced by 11 lifts, one reaching almost to the top of the 9,068-foot stratovolcano.

Winter adventures in Sunriver cover everything from cross-country skiing to snowmobile tours. The relatively flat meadow and surrounding areas are perfect for anyone looking for good cross-country skiing tracks. Mount Bachelor also offers 56 kilometers of machine-groomed and track-set trails for all cross-country skiers, with 69 percent of the trails rated "More Difficult." Several tour companies offer snowshoeing expeditions in and around Sunriver, and dog sledding and snowmobile trails are also available.

Sunriver was part of the course for the Atta Boy 300 Sled Dog race from 2002 to 2005. Sponsored by *The Bulletin*, the race attracted such stars as Iditarod champion Doug Swingley, as well as local star Rachel Scdoris, Central Oregon's all-time top young musher, who is also legally blind.

The Sunriver Brewing Company K-9 Keg Pull started in 2014 as part of the American Cancer Society's "Bark for Life" fundraising campaign. The 150-foot race is run every February at the Village in Sunriver. Based on weight, the dogs compete in six different categories, pulling everything from empty beer cans to full-size empty kegs. In 2018, the event drew over 160 dogs and their owners.

Nine

Hitting the High Note

Sunriver's premier cultural event is the annual Sunriver Music Festival, which brings top classical music talents to Central Oregon. Envisioned by a small group of classical music enthusiasts in 1976, the first music festival kicked off in August 1978. The enthusiasts behind the Sunriver Music Festival were Ray Fabrizio, a successful music teacher and one of the top flutists in America, and Sunriver residents Doug and Polly Kahle.

The principal founders were touring the Great Hall, when Mrs. Ray Fabrizio struck a few notes on the piano and Ray snapped his fingers. "Pretty good acoustics in here," said Ray, and someone else added, "Wouldn't it be a great place for a music festival?"

Jim Reeves, the manager of the Louisville Symphony, wrote out the proposal for arranging a music festival in the Great Hall and presented it to Sunriver Properties' publicity director Ann Wall. She loved the concept, and eventually, the developers/owners of Sunriver came onboard.

The first artistic director and conductor for the fledgling event was Lawrence Leighton Smith, who at the time was director of the Oregon Symphony.

The premiere concert featured "Beethoven, Brahms, and Bats," according to the Oregonian music critic Robert Lindstrom. "A furry flying friend who apparently makes his home in the Great Hall, where the concert was held, provided unscheduled entertainment by zooming over the heads of performers and audience."

Bach and Beethoven walk hand in hand with George Gershwin and world music. Over the years, the Sunriver Music Festival has stayed near to its classical music roots, even though it has expanded its fare to include family concerts, pops, solo recitals, and much more. To expand its base, Sunriver Music Festival has also made inroads in Bend. Since 2010, half of the festival has moved to Bend to make appearances at the Tower Theater and local high schools.

The event celebrated its 40th anniversary in 2017. The festival is financed through ticket sales, grants, donors, sponsors, and fundraisers.

The Sunriver Music Festival is an intimate affair. The concerts are held in the Great Hall, the grand mountain lodge commissioned by Colonel Besson in 1943. The Great Hall seats 400 people, and the festival's chamber orchestra is made up of roughly 40 musicians. In an August 2007 article in *The Bulletin*, then-former executive director Lori Noack, who headed the music festival from 1998 to 2005, said, "The Sunriver Music Festival is a niche boutique-type festival of the highest quality." The soldiers who built the officers' mess would have been proud their "training project" is still around and home to a classical music festival, weddings, and corporate banquets. (Below, courtesy of DHM.)

Smith resigned as Sunriver Music Festival's artistic director after the 1983 concert season and was replaced by several guest conductors including Sung Kwak, Seymour Lipkin, Gerhardt Zimmerman, and Murry Sidlin. Kwak stayed on for 10 seasons. In 1994, Smith returned after an invitation from the festival board and stayed until 2012, when he handed over the baton to the current artistic director, George Hanson (below). Originally hired as a guest conductor, Hanson was supposed to work with Smith during the 2011 season, but illness prevented Smith from traveling to Sunriver.

A testament to the popularity of classical music, the Sunriver Music Festival has remained in the black for most of its 40 years in business. This stability has created a feeling of a "family get-together" among the musicians who return to Sunriver every summer.

Principal oboe of Sunriver Music Festival since 1978, Peter Stempe is originally from Victorville, California, where he started his career as second oboe in the Victor Valley High School Jackrabbit Concert Band.

Sunriver Music Festival Valentine's Day Dinner and Concert is part of the Fireside Series, which features concerts from September through March. Away from the main summer festival, the concert series highlights classical and contemporary music. In February 2008, the Valentine's Day event featured Oregon singer-songwriter Tom Grant. Popular artists also included Sunriver Music Festival Young Artist Scholarship winners.

The music festival is also actively nurturing up-and-coming artists through the Young Artist Scholarship Program. The program started in 1996, and during the last 22 years, the Sunriver Music Festival has awarded nearly $475,000 in scholarships to local music students. Ben Lulich (right), a Young Artist alumnus from 2000, is currently principal clarinet of the Seattle Symphony. Here, he is pictured with Yo-Yo Ma.

Classical pianist Hunter Noack is a six-time Sunriver Music Festival Young Artist Scholarship winner. In December 2006, Noack returned to Sunriver to perform a concert at the Holy Trinity Church. "The festival has been one of the biggest influences of my life," he told the *Sunriver Scene*. After Sunriver, he studied music in Los Angeles and London. In 2018, his performance series "In a Landscape" was featured on Oregon Public Broadcasting.

Julia Hodecker is also a multiple Sunriver Music Festival Young Artist Scholarship recipient. She was awarded her first scholarship at the age of 12 and was a member of the Central Oregon Symphony from 2006 to her graduation in 2009.

Ten

The Sunriver Scene

In June 1993, the Los Angeles firm Lowes Enterprises Inc. completed its purchase of Sunriver from the previous owner, Connecticut Mutual Life Insurance Company. At the time, the Deschutes County assessor's office valued the Sunriver property at $23.6 million. A new company, Sunriver Resort Limited Partnership, was set up to manage the property.

Lowes Enterprises also purchased a 600-acre parcel from Connecticut Mutual Life Insurance Company south of Sunriver. The added acreage was set aside for a new nine-hole golf course as well as 94 homesites and 25 condominiums. Called Caldera Springs, the new development was further expanded in 2006 when Sunriver Resort Limited Partnership purchased an additional 614 acres from the federal government.

A majority of permanent Sunriver residents have over the years dreaded the word "incorporation." Meant to describe government-sanctioned operations to pay for city services such as police and fire departments, the issue was up for a vote in 1994, with permanent residents resoundingly voting down the effort. An earlier attempt in January 1992 was shot down by the Deschutes County Board of Commissioners. A little more than a year later, the Sunriver Incorporation Committee made a new push for incorporation, to no avail. Today, the community remains governed by a city council of sorts, which is made up of the SROA Board of Directors and the SROA.

Land ownership in Sunriver has been a complex issue for the community since its inception. Early on, the homeowners resisted any land swaps, but eventually their stance softened. A large land swap was negotiated in 1995 and more followed in 2000.

The pool closest to Sunriver Lodge was originally built by Sunriver Properties, but ownership was transferred to the SROA. In 2012, the 1.5-acre lot was traded back to Sunriver Resort for 33 acres, which included land close to Mary McCallum Park, river frontage, tennis courts, and land close to the SROA administration complex.

The community is constantly reminded of Camp Abbot's storied past. Old dog tags pop up in the high desert around Sunriver, residents find slivers of dinner plates from the Engineer Replacement Training Camp, and during the construction of SHARC, workers found both old wooden water pipes and plenty of asbestos in the ground.

Construction of Sunriver Lodge got under way in 1967 and was completed in 1969 at a cost of $1.7 million. After Lowes Enterprises acquired Sunriver Resort from Connecticut Mutual Life Insurance Company in 1993, the new owners undertook a $45 million renovation program, which included the lodge.

A $5.5 million renovation of Sunriver Lodge got under way in November 1997. The original lodge featured a Northwest or Cascadian-styled lodge. Thirty years later, the dark wood paneling and floors felt dated, according to Portland architect Tom Moisan, who handled the renovation. "We see the lodge as a modern classic, continuing in the rich tradition of Cascadian design," said Moisan in an interview with *The Bulletin*. (Courtesy of DHM.)

This Sunriver Lodge renovation focused on opening up the existing spaces and filling darkness with light. The architect added more skylights to the building, and the dark wood was promptly replaced with light pine wood. Along with the interior upgrades, the lodge received a much-needed exterior facelift, which included a new gable roof entry and a circular driveway. (Courtesy of DHM.)

The newly renovated lodge was reopened in early June 1998. The new entrance was adorned with slate floors, while the floor in the lobby and the rest of the public spaces was gutted and replaced with reclaimed antique pine floors, hand-forged iron railings, and custom rugs. To add to the Northwest theme, the architects commissioned numerous pieces of artwork to enhance public spaces. (Courtesy of DHM.)

The $50-million renovation of Sunriver Lodge continued in 2015 with a remodeling project that introduced locals and tourists to Carson's American Kitchen, Twisted River Tavern, and the great room between the two. In addition, Sunriver Resort replaced the old pool with a new facility called The Cove, a 3,200-square-foot pool, a raised hot tub, fire pits, and a restaurant and bar with outdoor seating. The owners of the resort also completed an update of all 245 lodge condos. "The New Sunriver Resort" was unveiled in mid-May 2015, while the official opening took place on Memorial Day. (Both, author's collection.)

It is not uncommon to hear classical music flowing throughout Sunriver Lodge. Promoting Sunriver Festival of Music, acclaimed Young Artist Program musicians perform in intimate settings.

Sunriver Lodge has become the winter headquarters for Sunriver Traditions, a sparkling holiday event that features horse-drawn sleigh rides, seasonal music, visits from Santa and Mrs. Claus, and Central Oregon's largest display of holiday lights. It takes over 375,000 individual holiday lights strung together to light up the lodge. And Santa's elves bake 6,000 sugar cookies and over 4,000 gingerbread cookies for the event.

Sunriver is home to a blossoming shopping district called The Village at Sunriver, which features fine dining, local arts and crafts, a bookstore, a hardware store, a bank, a candy store, several real estate offices, the Sunriver Chamber of Commerce, the post office, and a large outdoor skating rink. Included in the mall area are 14 acres of undeveloped land, and there have been many attempts to develop the area for housing. So far, the efforts have failed. Today, The Village at Sunriver is owned by Rediscover Sunriver Village. The current owners have set out on an ambitious upgrade and redevelopment project. (Below, author's collection.)

Early residents of Sunriver remember a time when groceries had to be purchased outside of the community and transported in by car. Resupplying meant a trip to Bend. That changed in 1972, when businessman Joe Audia opened the Sunriver Country Store. It was actually the first business in the Sunriver Village Mall development. Originally housed in a smaller building, Audia settled into the current space in 1984. The store has gone through many reconstruction and remodeling projects. In May 2011, Joe Audia and his son John unveiled the current look of the store. The picture at right shows, from left to right, SROA's Hugh Palcic, store owner John Audia and his father Joe, and Dennis Smeage of the Sunriver Chamber of Commerce.

A life-long love affair with books and music is the back-story for Sunriver Books & Music. Owners Deon and Richard Stonehouse—and their canine executive officer, Flashman—opened the bookstore in 2005. Over the years, the Stonehouses have hosted many evenings with notable authors. Craig Johnson (pictured), author of the Walt Longmire novels, is a frequent visitor, as is famous local author Jane Kirkpatrick.

Who does not want to wet their whistle on a hot summer day? The craft brew craze is sweeping the Central Oregon landscape. Every town on the high desert sports its own craft brewery, and Sunriver is no exception. Sunriver Brewing Company, a family-owned brewpub, started drawing hand-crafted beer on July 4, 2012.

The annual Sunriver Quilt Show has gathered a following since 1988, when the Mountain Meadow Quilters and the Sunriver Village Mall turned the shopping area into an outdoor exhibit. The organization counts over 100 members, who meet monthly for quilting and spirited conversations. In 2018, over 200 quilts were on display, with many offered for sale. Mountain Meadow Quilters supports a wide range of nonprofit organizations in the area.

Many Sunriver residents and visiting "chili heads" have fond memories of the annual Sunriver Chili Cookoff. The event drew connoisseurs from all over the Pacific Northwest, who prepared their own versions of red-hot chili. Over the years, many famous judges presided over the cookoff. World War II veteran and chili enthusiast "Buffalo Jim" Yaple was featured as one of the judges at the Chili Cookoff in 1988.

With unprecedented fishing opportunities nearby, it is no surprise that Sunriver has an Angler's Club. The organization made its first appearance along the Deschutes River in 1976, and the club has been going strong ever since. The Members of the Angler's Club are strong supporters of a healthy river, partnering with the Oregon Department of Fish and Wildlife in upgrading river habitat and tributary fisheries.

The Sunriver Women's Club (SRWC) has been an active participant in the community since 1976. The club is open to all women in Sunriver and surrounding communities. Recognizing that many residents of South Deschutes County have significant needs for basic necessities, philanthropy has been the main focus of the organization. The SRWC has awarded over $500,000 in grants to local area nonprofits since 1999.

The former South Pool area was transformed into Besson Commons on Saturday, September 7, 2013, to honor Col. Frank S. Besson, who commanded Camp Abbot during World War II. At the dedication of the outdoor venue, almost 70 years after the dedication of the officers' mess, distinguished guests unveiled a memorial plaque. Inscribed on the plaque is a quote by Colonel Besson from the dedication of the officers' mess on April 29, 1944: "In every theater of war, the Engineers are using their tools and their weapons with equal skill. Let us continue with our efforts of training soldiers who are the 'first ones in and the last ones out' when the going is toughest." Pictured above from left to right are Gene Whisnant, Oregon House of Representatives; Frank Besson III, Colonel Besson's grandson; and Tom O'Shea, Sunriver Resort managing director. Below, the founder of Bend Heroes Foundation, Lt. Col. Dick Tobiason, addresses the gathered visitors.

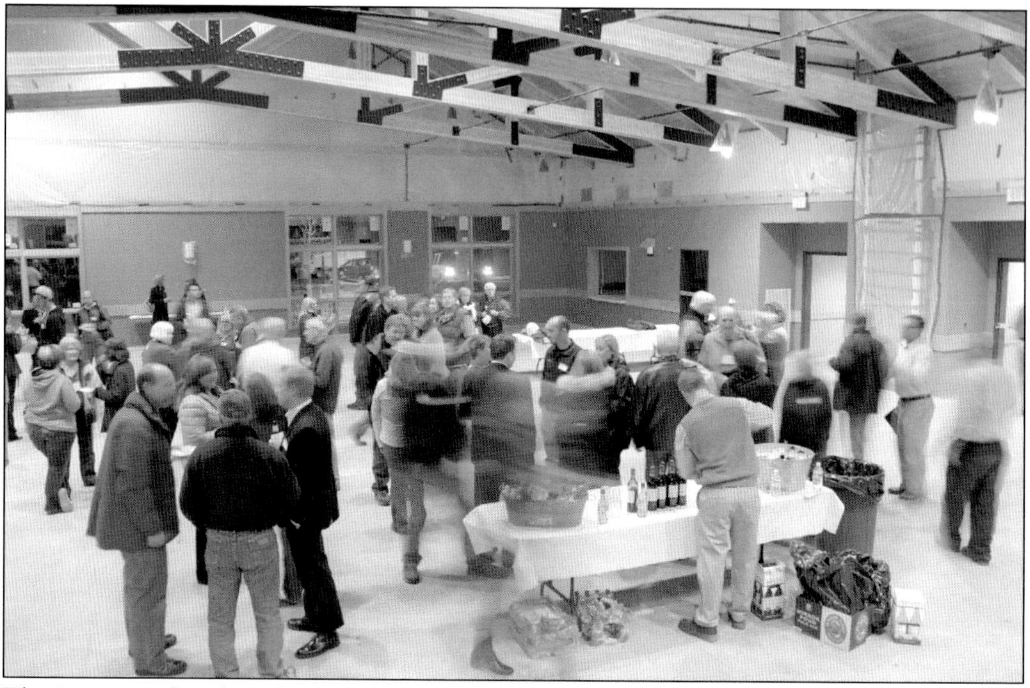

The Sunriver Chamber of Commerce was founded in 1987 by people who believed Sunriver was the ideal place to run a business. The chamber is also supporting the idea "Think Local, Buy Local" in an effort to keep money in the community. The chamber has more than 200 members. Over the years, its focus has been to attract "environmentally clean" businesses to the community. The Sunriver Business Park was originally owned by Sunriver Properties. The first building was constructed in 1974. Over the years, the business park has become an integral part of the community, not only for over 60 local businesses, but also as the home of Three Rivers School, the Sunriver Post Office, and the Sunriver Library, which is a part of the Deschutes Public Library.

Sunriver's airport is one of the busier general aviation airports in Oregon. Homeowners and visitors fly in to spend a couple of days enjoying the peace and quiet. The airport is managed by Sunriver Resort. The original airstrip was upgraded and expanded in 1985 when the runway was lengthened to 5,500 feet to accommodate multi-engine and jet aircraft. The airport was also upgraded with a visual approach slope indicator lighting system. In April 2009, the runway was widened from 70 to 75 feet and repaved to accommodate heavier aircraft. The $720,000 project was funded by Destination Hotels & Resorts, which owns Sunriver Resort. Steve Runner, vice president of development, told *The Bulletin*, "Sunriver Airport will be considered among the region's finest private runways." The airport terminal is open 24 hours a day but staffed only during daytime.

Maintaining a "defensible space" is more than a catchphrase for Sunriver residents. The community's homeowners got a heavy-handed wake-up call when the Awbrey Hall Fire swept through the western edges of Bend in 1990. The loss of 22 homes, mainly in the Sunrise Village subdivision, reminded Sunriver homeowners of the dangers of living in a forested community. Among the lessons learned was that many of the homes destroyed by the fire could have been saved by simply maintaining "defensible space." In 1996, after the Skeleton Fire swept through a southeastern Bend neighborhood, Bend fire marshal Gary Marshall introduced the FireFree Program, 10 steps to protect homes from wildfires. Originally the Covenants, Codes, and Restrictions (CC&R) for the community of Sunriver stated that homes were to have wooden shake roofs in an effort to maintain a "natural look." After the destructive Bend fires, the SROA rethought its position and relaxed the CC&Rs to allow for metal, tile, or other fire-resistant roofing material to be used in new construction. Homeowners quickly replaced fire-prone shake roofs with modern material.

The Sunriver Police Department's bike patrols are out in force during the busy summer months. Mainly keeping Sunriver's bike population safe, the officers make sure helmets are worn and lights on bikes are in working order. In cooperation with the SROA, Sunriver police also conduct a bike path safety program for kids.

The popular Sunriver Police Academy program helps Sunriver citizens understand what it takes to be a police officer. The program is open to both women and men. The academy is a series of seminars to teach Sunriver residents about law enforcement. Classes include a visit to the Deschutes County Jail and the 911 Emergency Dispatch Center in Bend, hands-on classes in firearms safety, and how to spot an intoxicated driver.

Sunriver features many unique homes. The owners of nine Skypark homes can land at the airport, taxi off the runway, and roll their planes into their home's attached hangar. Here are Chris and Millie Christensen outside their home with their Piper PA-18-150. The Skypark homes are complemented with 30 privately owned hangars, which can accommodate most any type of general aviation aircraft.

With nearly 300 days of blue skies and sun, the developers had a good idea about the weather when they named the community Sunriver. Paul Sobel's passive solar home was built in 1981. Sobel taught alternative energy courses at Pima College in Tucson, Arizona, and put his expertise into constructing his Sunriver home. Sobel estimates he saves about 60 percent on his utility bills.

The community has been served by its own newsletter/newspaper, originally named the *Harold*, since 1977. A photocopied four-page newsletter at the start, it has grown to become a monthly newspaper called the *Sunriver Scene*, which averages 40 pages covering just about everything that goes on in Sunriver. Under the slogan "Take A Trip, Take A Scene, Take A Picture," the *Sunriver Scene* has traveled around the world thanks to enthusiastic Sunriver residents and visitors to the resort community.

Bibliography

The Bend Bulletin and *The Bulletin*. Various articles, 1942–2018.

Lucas, Peggy Chessman. *Mount Bachelor: Bill Healy's Dream: the History and Development of Mount Bachelor Ski Resort*. Bend, OR: Maverick Publications, 1999.

Cressman, Luther Sheeleigh. *The Sandal and the Cave: The Indians of Oregon*. Corvallis, OR: Oregon State University Press, 2005.

Hanson, Tor. *Camp Abbot*. Charleston, SC: Arcadia Publishing, 2018.

Haynes, Ted, and Grace Vandevert McNellis. *Vandevert: The Hundred Year History of a Central Oregon Ranch*. Menlo Park, CA: Robleda, 2011.

Joslin, Les. *Deschutes National Forest*. Charleston, SC: Arcadia Publishing, 2017.

Quinn, James W. *Sunriver: The First 20 Years*. Medford, OR: Commercial Printing Co., 1990.

INDEX